The First House

The First House

Myth, Paradigm, and the Task of Architecture

R. D. Dripps

The MIT Press
Cambridge, Massachusetts
London, England

© 1997 Massachusetts Institute of Technology

This book was set in Baskerville by Graphic Composition, Inc., and was printed and bound in the United States of America.

Library of Congress Cataloging-in-Publication Data

Dripps, R. D.
    The first house : myth, paradigm, and the task of architecture /
R. D. Dripps.
      p.   cm.
    ISBN 0-262-04163-4
    1. Architecture—Philosophy.   2. Architecture and society.
I. Title.
NA2500.D75   1997
720'.1—dc21
                                    97-8889
                                        CIP

For Lionel, mapmaker and planner of imaginary cities

Contents

Preface

In writing this book I am imagining that architecture can once again find itself at the center of an inclusive intellectual, political, and artistic debate. This is exactly the position that Vitruvius imagined when he produced the first architectural treatise, and this intention persisted through the early twentieth century when Le Corbusier produced the most recent work within this continuing project.

The disengaged or reductive quality of current architectural discourse unfortunately does not seem to produce arguments and theories sufficiently broad in scope and adventuresome to continue to address important political, cultural, and ecological issues. Thoughts, actions, and artifacts appear to be floating freely, with no apparent engagement with the intellectual and physical world they must have come from and which one would hope they might help to direct. Without a connection to the immense intellectual project of understanding the world and our place within it, thinking closes in on itself, producing hypotheses that are increasingly autonomous, hermetic, and diminished in reach.

The purpose of this book is to describe a larger landscape in order to provide a picture of the full range of issues that one is able to address as an architect. The potentially vast territory of discourse, however, is so dense with the landmarks of previous explorers that orientation is always difficult to maintain. It is useful to describe such a large world of action by reference to a very small and seemingly simplistic story. Vitruvius's imaginative myth of the origins of dwelling is a story of urban humanity at its most basic level. By looking very carefully at this small tale and making our own hypotheses about its critique of the world, we can open a path from which to survey the immense intellectual territory extending between Vitruvius and ourselves. By its help we can follow the labyrinthine routes of the many scholars who have been pioneers in this area, and can extend their work into the present.

I hope that in at least a few instances, I can rescue both ideas and the people associated with these from their unfortunate captivity within history. So much important thinking has been consumed and discarded as no longer relevant to our advancing present that our context lacks the depth and breadth crucial to the consideration of matters of importance. The traces that remain are designated as historical, therefore outside of the ongoing process of making hypotheses about the world. I have thus consistently addressed Vitruvius as if he were present today. I firmly believe that his thoughts are still capable of contributing to an expanding discourse.

This book is structured as a series of explorations of Vitruvius's myth of architectural beginnings. The first chapter develops the elemental geometric patterning of Vitruvius's account (center and periphery, secure inside and untamed outside, the vertical stance of the human subject) as a diagram both for the private house and for the public space of the city. The second chapter examines the power of paradigmatic structures—both architectural and intellectual—to represent order and authority in human affairs. The third explores architecture's capacity to represent the public realm, and through representation to help effect public action. Chapter 4 seeks to reestablish connections between architectural order and the order of the cosmos, working back from myth-making to its significance for architectural and urbanistic practice. The final chapter addresses the task of constructing as a part of public life, while a brief epilogue proposes a revision of the Vitruvian myth in the light of modern ecological thought.

As this book aims to provide a base for a larger landscape for architectural action, both productive and theoretical, I have included extensive notes that point outward in various directions. These notes serve to counter the sense of disconnection and claustrophobia that might be brought on by such intense reliance on Vitruvius's small tale. There is a larger world implied by this tale, and the tale is a point of embarkation from which one may pursue many tangents. The analyses and quotations incorporated in the notes are intended to provide direction for readers pursuing their own investigations of these ideas.

Acknowledgments

This book is a collaborative project, the direct consequence of the larger project of teaching. I therefore wish to recognize the importance of my own teachers, my teaching colleagues, the students who have made this possible, and those teachers, though we have met only through their books and essays, who have influenced my thinking at a distance.

At the beginning of both my studies in architecture and their careers in teaching, Michael Graves and Peter Eisenman opened to me an understanding of a potential within this discipline that has sustained my efforts to the present. Both introduced me to the value of the important literature in architecture at a time when reading about architecture was considered by many a strange activity. My understanding of the city as the critical context for architecture was the result of their directing, albeit under cover, my senior thesis at Princeton.

Teaching architecture is a very special kind of teaching. Without the challenge of having constantly to articulate a point of view, to question the views of one's colleagues, to admit error, and above all to do this in public, this book could never have been written. In many respects teaching in a school of architecture comes close to the example of "building and boasting" that Vitruvius shows occurring in the deliberative assembly of people who initiated and developed the ideas at the foundation of civilization and of architecture. There are many teachers who have in their own way contributed to this project, but in particular I want to thank Bruce Abbey, Alan Colquhoun, Michael

Dennis, Elizabeth Meyer, Demetri Porphyrios, Jaquelin Robertson, Tom Schumacher, Sam Stevens, Nancy Takahashi, Robert Jan Van Pelt, Peter Waldman, and Carroll William Westfall.

I have been fortunate in working with a body of students who over the years have been the true inspiration for everything in this book. Most important are those I have worked with as they investigated some aspect of our discipline through the thesis project. This is the most intense form of educational commitment that students and faculty can enter into, and the discussions and revelations have been crucial to all my work. Among many memorable students, several stand out as particularly significant to the ideas of this book: Bethany Christensen, Julie Gabrielli, Amy Gardner, Mason Disosway, Alan Dynerman, Kate Hanenberg, Susan Pikaart-Bristol, Donna Robertson, Erik Thorkildsen, Katherine Willson, and Jill Gilliand who showed me the first subtractive diagram.

The scholarship of the many teachers who have made their insights available through their books, articles, and lectures has provided the intellectual foundation for most of my own research. I would like to acknowledge in particular Robin Evans, Kenneth Frampton, J. B. Jackson, Colin Rowe, and Joseph Rykwert.

The diagrams and drawings that demonstrate some of the ideas of the book were produced by Celia Liu. That these could be so successful owes in part to Celia's own critical role as a teacher while operating as my teaching assistant in a seminar on the ideas of this book.

I would also like to acknowledge the help and insights of Julie Gabrielli, Lucia Phinney, and Francisco Sanin, who read early drafts of the text and offered necessary advice, and Schaeffer Somers for his meticulous checking of bibliographical sources.

The sensitive and elegant editing of the final text by Matthew Abbate (he described this as pruning the undergrowth) contributed greatly to the clarity with which these ideas have been presented.

Finally, this book should be acknowledged as a collaborative effort between myself and Lucia Phinney. All the ideas I am writing about are a result of a twenty-year continuing discussion on the scope of architecture. The many ideas that she brought to this book, the particular structure of many of its arguments, and her unique understanding of the land have been crucial to both my teaching and this text.

The First House

"Therefore it was the discovery of fire that originally gave rise to the coming together of men, to the deliberative assembly, and to social intercourse." *Drawing by Celia Liu.*

1

The Origin of Dwelling

Early in *The Ten Books of Architecture,* yet following a section devoted to the location and layout of the city, Vitruvius describes the origin of the first dwelling. The account is impressive for the breadth of the intertwined themes that are implicated in bringing this house into being. At least as much narrative weight is given to establishing the events and actions that constituted the context for this house as is devoted to the house itself. As his treatise supplies no illustrations, we are further distanced from this artifact and more taken by the process of its becoming. What Vitruvius describes is not merely the making of a detached and autonomous artifact but the origins of political structure, the formation of language, and finally the birth of architecture. This architecture, surprisingly, is not self-conscious about its external image. Rather, attention is directed toward the rituals of its making and eventual habitation. There is a profound interiority to what Vitruvius describes. These are internally experienced volumes, or places that house the human figure whose imprint is a constant presence. Vitruvius's fable is about a prearchitectural state of ritual action directed toward establishing orientation, order, and stability in the world.

If it is still possible to consider this story as a paradigm, then its validity should be measured against the most general ideas and actions that underlie the making of architecture. (This process of validation would be in contrast to that proposed by Marc-Antoine Laugier in his *Essay on Architecture,* whose more visually satisfying hut was intended as a model to be replicated. Although Laugier's hut prospered as the exemplar of a classical revival, its value has been so linked to the circumstances of a particular historical moment that it has lingered on more as a product of historical speculation than as a general guide to the making of architecture.) Vitruvius's story offers us much, yet what is offered is perplexingly enigmatic. Are facts that we extract too local and archaic to be the basis of subsequent first principles? Aside from these facts, we find several tenuously connected anecdotal fragments. Are these remote from any current understanding of the world? It is precisely because Vitruvius moves outside of history that these anecdotal fragments register as mythic and archetypal, and as such can sustain examination under circumstances that, on the surface, appear to be totally different.

The Ten Books of Architecture was written specifically for the use of the emperor Augustus. Vitruvius addresses Augustus as he "was now giving his attention not only to the welfare of society in general and to the establishment of public order, but also to the providing of public buildings intended for utilitarian purposes, so that not only should the state have been enriched with provinces by your means, but that the greatness of its power might likewise be attended with distinguished authority in its public buildings."[1] He leaves little doubt that architecture has both a public agenda and a political purpose. Vitruvius wrote about the dwelling only after he had commented on the siting and layout of the city in Book One. The city and the house, or the place of gathering and the dwelling for the individual human being, are thus engaged in an intense relationship that is fundamental to this discourse on architecture. The import of the dedication to Augustus becomes evident in the account of the origins of the first dwelling in Book Two:

1. The men of old were born like the wild beasts, in woods, caves, and groves, and lived on savage fare. As time went on, the thickly crowded trees in a certain place, tossed by storms and winds, and rubbing their branches against one another, caught fire, and so the inhabitants of the place were put to flight, being terrified by the furious flame. After it subsided, they drew near, and observing that they were very comfortable standing before the warm fire, they put on logs and, while thus keeping it alive, brought up other people to it, showing them by signs how much comfort they got from it. In that gathering of men, at a time when utterance of sound was purely individual, from daily

habits they fixed upon articulate words just as these had happened to come;
then, from indicating by name things in common use, the result was that in
this chance way they began to talk, and thus originated conversation with
one another.

2. Therefore it was the discovery of fire that originally gave rise to the coming together of men, to the deliberative assembly, and to social intercourse.
And so, as they kept coming together in greater numbers into one place, finding themselves naturally gifted beyond the other animals in not being obliged
to walk with faces to the ground, but upright, and gazing upon the splendor
of the starry firmament, and also in being able to do with ease whatever they
chose with their hands and fingers, they began in that first assembly to construct shelters. Some made them of green boughs, others dug caves on mountain sides, and some, in imitation of the nests of swallows and the way they
built, made places of refuge out of mud and twigs. Next, by observing the
shelters of others and adding new details to their own inceptions, they constructed better and better kinds of huts as time went on.

3. And since they were of an imitative and teachable nature, they would
daily point out to each other the results of their building, boasting of the novelties in it; and thus, with their natural gifts sharpened by emulation, their standards improved daily. At first they set up forked stakes connected by twigs
and covered these walls with mud. Others made walls of lumps of dried mud,
covering them with reeds and leaves to keep out the rain and the heat. Finding
that such roofs could not stand the rain during the storms of winter, they built
them with peaks daubed with mud, the roofs sloping and projecting so as to
carry off the rain water.[2]

The fire whose cause was so laconically described becomes a critical
datum dividing human existence into a prepolitical state of the individual and the political structure of gathering. There is little doubt
about the quality of life before the fire. Although devoted almost exclu-
sively to the basic needs for survival, this life must have been quite
successful and perfectly satisfactory; otherwise the primitive human
beings would never have appeared at the scene of the fire. This was,
however, a life of individuals, a private life. Public action was unknown
and therefore language was unnecessary. There was no political entity,
there was no culture, and without these there was no architecture.

This contrasts with the condition presented after the fire. While the
contingency of the fire, an act of fate, brought these individuals together, it was the "deliberative assembly" growing out of this that in-
dicated the development of a public consciousness. Nothing had
changed functionally because of the fire: the same tasks had to be

performed in order to survive. What *did* change was the recognition of the value of public action. Discourse arose when individual utterance gave way to the naming of things in common use. This was not an instrumental use of language. No suggestion is made that advantage might accrue relative to matters of survival. Vitruvius offers only the desire to communicate the comfort of being near the fire as the instigation for this beginning of language.

Vitruvius is describing much more than the first dwelling. Or, perhaps, the idea of dwelling is a more profound and involved concept than the making of shelter. Dwelling, for Vitruvius, is part of the public life of the city. As we can see, the dwelling, although distinct from the "deliberative assembly" or place of gathering, is fully engaged as a part of this gathering. Dwelling and gathering form a political and architectural bond that together defines the essential idea of the public realm. It is notable then that among the Romans for whom Vitruvius writes, "to live" and "to be among men" were phrases that could be interchanged one for the other.[3] For those more accustomed to the now current view of the house as a private refuge with no relationship to the public realm, Vitruvius's proposal poses a significant challenge, one that would relocate the dwelling appropriately at the center of public life. And so this first dwelling, now removed from the privacy of the woods, caves, and forests in order to engage in public life, transcends the contingent demands of shelter to become architecture.

Language plays a critical role in this transformation. Its absence before the fire was all the evidence needed by Vitruvius to establish the deprivations of the solitary life of the individual within the forest. Without speech, a person is unable to become a political being. Conversely, the transformation from individual utterance to conversation among people could never have taken place privately. It demanded the presence of others, a public. Speech is a public activity that results from the coming together of people. This coming together is where the uniqueness and singularity of the individual can be tested and compared with the plurality of the collective. This is where one comes to terms with what it means to be a human being and therefore where one begins to understand the world.

Language, however, has an even more profound influence on the human being's world. Without speech we are incapable of thought and are without the ability to plan.[4] Consequently our activities are limited to behavioral necessity rather than purposeful action. As speech rises out of the gathering of people, it transcends instrumentality. It no longer is simply one of the facilities among many that distinguish the human condition, rather speech is coterminous with reason itself.[5]

Vitruvius acknowledges this status of language when he describes the naming of things as an intermediate stage between individual utterance and meaningful public discourse. How could this be otherwise? Thinking and words go together. Irrespective of the direction of causality, ideas are fixed in our mind by means of words. Vitruvius's primitive people therefore "fixed upon articulate words just as these had happened to come" and only then proceeded to the naming of things in common use. The thought of words preceding and existing independent of their referents is unexpected. It reverses the positivist stance that words are a direct outcome of an instrumental functionality and, therefore, that the need itself precedes its sign.[6] Vitruvius is suggesting that words are formed as a consequence of some capacity innate within each human being. These words are then shared by all, and only later are words employed in satisfaction of some need.

The import of this early hypothesis on the formation of language and its conjunction with the formation of architecture raises the possibility that architecture, like the word, might have an autonomous existence independent of external contingency. And just as the word assumes its greatest import in the speech that rises out of the gathering of people trying to understand the world, might not the value of architecture similarly be found in the relationships it establishes between these people and their world?[7]

The Ten Books of Architecture is situated in a precarious position between history and the timeless independence of myth.[8] Later writers, critical of its apparent contradictions and lapses in narrative structure and writing under historical and intellectual conditions far removed from Augustan Rome, have increasingly tended to deemphasize the importance of its mythic subtext, eventually ignoring it altogether as they carried the theory of architecture into a post Enlightenment world. Vitruvius, however, has an ambitious project in mind: the making of an architecture that while responsive to both political and material contingency aspires to the universal and timeless. While the former is easily described within the conventions of historical narrative, the latter is problematic. How does one describe something timeless and universal (having no fixed place) and escape the paradox that the descriptive mechanisms themselves are likely to implicate a definite temporal moment and a particular spatial location? Vitruvius's solution is to move outside of time and history and draw on the processes and structures of mythical thinking.[9] Unlike history, which to a greater degree is dependent on external cause, myth gains in objectivity as it remains indifferent to external causation, divesting itself of accident in order to demonstrate universal principle. And unlike empirical thought, which tends to take the world apart leaving its pieces as disembodied fragments, myth strives to apprehend a unity of the world and expects this to be the consequence of purposive action.

But Vitruvius's tale is not pure myth. He presents a form of collage that incorporates mythic fragments with the apparent facts of history. The mention of the actual locatons of Marseilles and Athens, for instance, is enough to establish a known historical context. The subsequent details of local building practice that Vitruvius describes are therefore historically grounded more by inference than fact, which frees them to participate in the myth that he is weaving. By dislocating actions both spatially and temporally from a historical context, he gains the autonomy needed to elevate these actions to an ideal state. And since they commingle with historical actuality, these actions begin to endow history with a purpose that otherwise it would lack. The contradictions in the text are therefore likely to be a consequence of the deliberate juxtaposition of two different narrative intentions, the historic and the mythic, whose proximity can definitely be troubling.

The scope of the Vitruvian project becomes evident as he continues to describe that first dwelling. Again, architecture is explicitly situated in the public realm as "they began in that first assembly to construct shelters." Up to this point the place of assembly has been included in the story in order to establish and qualify a relationship between dwelling and gathering and to suggest a public purpose for the house as it participates in the making of the public realm. But there is something else on Vitruvius's mind. After establishing this place of political action he brings it more centrally to the making of architecture itself.

The Origin of Dwelling

Conditioned by subsequent treatises, we might well be anticipating here a description, perhaps in detail, of a building rendered in a specific and ideologically correct style, but Vitruvius offers scant indication on matters of style. Instead he offers a series of clues in the form of poetic tropes and mythic fragments connoting specific archetypal conditions and a narration of process by which architecture, beginning as an idea, develops from the necessarily vague and indescribable status of archetype to a fully realized artifact. This process is accompanied by, and responsive to, the ever-increasing self-awareness and political sophistication of an engaged public audience. Consider the following lines:

Finding themselves naturally gifted beyond the other animals in not being obliged to walk with faces to the ground, but upright, and gazing upon the splendor of the starry firmament . . . they began in that first assembly to construct shelters. . . . Next, by observing the shelters of others and adding new details to their own inceptions, they constructed better and better kinds of huts as time went on. And since they were of an imitative and teachable nature, they would daily point out to each other the results of their building, boasting of the novelties in it; and thus, with their natural gifts sharpened by emulation, their standards improved daily.

The simplicity of these lines is in striking contrast to the complexity of their intent. When Vitruvius includes the upright figure gazing on the starry firmament, he is speculating on the characteristics of an inherited spatial reasoning that will become the foundation for all subsequent architectural action. He goes further: these characteristics, forming the structure by which one human might attempt to make sense of the world, are little more than abstractions until such a person participates in the political and artistic life of society. This participation occurs in an accretive process whereby the individual's inventive response to contingent demands and expressive initiative are publicly measured. If judged successful, the result can be added to a growing body of public example. We find that Vitruvius is describing how standards are established and how they are advanced.

Two conditions for making architecture are thus distinguished: a first moment or origin and a process of elaboration and transformation, which curiously brings to this otherwise evanescent beginning a fleeting sense of the concrete as a more definite form emerges in response to the context.

These first huts changed slowly and deliberately and even then only a part at a time. Vitruvius almost suggests a familiarity with the methods of modern scientific research, where variables are limited so as to define exactly how something under investigation will respond to a new stimulus. This is highly rationalized action now being described, as reason has taken over from intuition as a guide for invention. Moreover, it is interesting to find invention attached to the transformation and elaboration of architecture rather than to its inception. Of course this is expected, for how could people invent their origins? If origins were subject to the latitude of choice implied by invention, then little comfort could be derived from the resulting variety of interpretations. No, what is being offered is the hope that the apparently bewildering condition of the present might be traced back to a common beginning more stable and more powerful.

This retracing to a point of origin needs clarification. This is a speculative rather than an archaeological project. We would be naive to imagine that we might uncover actual evidence and imprudent to think that, if we could, the contingent nature of this discovery would offer anything of universal or lasting value. The object of our inquiry is not the rustic hut itself, an artifact whose actuality could only be the most banal of treasures, but nothing less than the origin of dwelling. If it were otherwise, architecture, rather than becoming richly diffuse in its elaborative response to a developing culture, would forever be reduced to a simple sign of itself.

Now the implications of the activities of these imitative and teachable first architects seem clear. In making architecture they are producing artifacts and settings that are as revealing of an ideal past as they are prophetic about the ability for present action to continue into the future. But rather than leaving the past, present, and future disconnected and alien to each other, I would propose that the Vitruvian protagonists, with their pointing, boasting, and finally building, were creating an architecture that could give structure and meaning to universal and enduring relationships, explaining and qualifying the passage from an ideal past into the future. This temporal ligature, serving as the foundation for a program of transformation and elaboration, is embedded in the very fabric of architecture, becoming its primary expressive content.

We have already been told that the people of the first society fixed on articulate words and only later constructed their language. Might not architecture furnish a parallel account? I have already noted that building became architecture, much the way individual utterance became first words and then speech, as it moved from the solitary privacy of the forest into the clearing and the subsequent public assembly. I am hesitant to overextend this linguistic analogy, but it is difficult not to suppose that Vitruvius, in first demonstrating the necessity of the presence of a public for the development of speech, is equally interested in a discursive process for the development of architecture.[10] Surely this is the aim of all the pointing to, imitating, and boasting; activities that would hold little meaning if done alone.[11]

What might we make of this tale so far? An architecture claiming archetypal authority by virtue of its imitation of an origin promises the most stable foundation for human existence. Yet if architecture were only concerned with the recovery of a moment of origin, a moment universal and fundamental to all subsequent architecture, then its degree of specificity would be so diminished that it would fail to provide any compelling guide to the present. The security of authority would become a constraint, discouraging the invention demanded to contend with the new. On the other hand, if architecture were nothing more than a consequence of immediate contingency, it could not initiate and develop the inherent structures and paradigms that, with their stability and capacity to order, are able to resist and comprehend the rapid and bewildering change that is the necessary condition of the present.

Vitruvius's conflation of history and myth promises a more satisfactory role for architecture. In this conflation the diffuse realities of the present coexist with the concentrated intensity surrounding the foundation of the world. If architecture can offer some meaningful and accessible causality between these, then the past becomes liberating in the process of revealing a hopeful present.

The Diagram of the First Dwelling

Vitruvius's treatise was unillustrated. While speculation on the form of the first house has been a part of most subsequent architectural treatises, virtually all of these present a concrete example, fully documented through drawings. If we try to picture the Vitruvian hut, an image arises new to us each time we summon it to mind. Compared to the many huts already rendered complete through illustration (thereby demanding little involvement on our part), an image that can only be recovered through our imagination is much more persuasive. The Vitruvian image becomes compelling and immediate precisely because its sketchiness requires us to fill in what is missing. We participate in an imaginative reconstruction combining the particulars of our own lives and accumulated experience with the ideal state of his universal, unchanging tale.[12]

There is another important point on which this account differs from its followers. The latter seem concerned to a greater degree either with the external characteristics of the hut as an object, a thing, or with the details of its construction and method of assembly. Vitruvius is more interested in the hut as constructed manifestation of the rituals of dwelling that are requisite for human habitation. This is not a representation of a house, but a place that accommodates and promotes the act of dwelling. It is because of these differences that one can outline a diagram of Vitruvius's first dwelling while avoiding the problems that ensue when one attempts a specific illustration of the hut.

I wish to use this term *diagram* in a very particular manner: arrived at through a process of simplification, it is a form of geometrical code that indicates the structure or system of relationships inherent to some action, object, or place and presents this from a particular point of view. An important characteristic of the diagram is its dependence on the principles of geometry. Geometry, used as metaphor, establishes the significance of the relationship between the structure of human action and the concomitant structure of the place where this action is enabled and made manifest. The simple elegance of the diagram belies the complexity of explanation available to it. The almost elemental clarity that is its most conspicuous feature should not be mistaken for a reductive image, an impoverished substitute. Rather, the diagram commands a structural logic and integrity of its own that parallels and even rivals the object of its imitation as it simultaneously reveals what otherwise might remain hidden within this object.

There is much in common between the diagram, in this sense, and the Vitruvian tale itself. Both are striving for the essence of an idea that in the richness of its varied and often competing implications eludes common description. In both there is an intensity at the core that provides the structure necessary for its own stability as well as for the elaborative qualifications that might otherwise tend to destabilize it. And both become open to the possibility of further elaboration and qualification by the deciphering that is implied in its presentation. Like the diagram, Vitruvius's mythic account is intensely concerned with matters of situation and structure. The diagram is, in fact, an analogue to mythic thinking.

Consider first the spatial structure that we might extract from the public setting for that first deliberative assembly of people: it is a clearing in the forest that has the fire at its center.[13] A more simple diagram would be difficult to imagine, yet the promise of intention latent within it is great. The constituent parts are few: a marking of center (the fire), the circumscribed boundary that delimits the domain over which this center holds influence, the horizontal ground plane that is marked off by this edge, and finally the roof, which defines the possible relationships between this place and the sky. Yet one would need little additional information in order to establish the foundation structure for most human settlements.

The clearing with its circular boundary is an ideal form as it takes on the archetypal nature of its foundation. Vitruvius therefore provides no topographical or otherwise contingent qualification. Under these circumstances the circle is appropriate, since its own geometrical foundation is so perfect: a radius is the only knowledge needed for its construction, and its most obvious manifestation, the circumference, is completely undifferentiated, offering total resistance to deformation. Furthermore, its point of origin, the center, is always implied by the circumference. It seems obvious why this figure has been persistently used to represent the most important tasks of civilization.[14]

Starting then with this bounded figure, recognizable and measurable as it demarcates a place distinct from its chaotic surroundings, we might be equally impressed that it still remains ambiguous. Is this the tangible edge of the forest, and therefore of the pre-pyric private world of the solitary individual, mute in the absence of speech? Might it be the more implied edge made by the assembled people as they gather around the fire, their radius dependent on the radiating warmth and light of the fire?[15] Or might both descriptions be true, the resultant redundancy a reflection of the complex reciprocity between forest and clearing?[16]

The unequivocal focus of this boundary is the fire. Its importance is initially guaranteed by its ability to protect the assembly from physical attack; then it provides the warmth and light that draw people together. Finally, consequent to this purposive assembly, the fire takes on a totemic role. It reminds us of the distance that has been achieved relative to the wilderness, yet simultaneously reveals the immediacy of that same wild nature which was the source of the fire.

The horizontal ground plane bounded by this figure is the most immediately experienced of the elements of the diagram. It is on this surface, measured by the rhythmic tread of the foot, that a person carries out the organized activities of public life. The irregularities of this rough earthen surface are diminished as the ground is leveled to accommodate particular human movements, allowing these to be compared to the more distant datum of the horizon. Finally, since our diagram must not be without the volumetric implications that are so evident in the story, there is the canopy of the sky, the celestial soffit.

Wall, terrace, hearth, and roof; these are the fundamental components of virtually all subsequent reconstitutions of the primitive hut. It is critical that Vitruvius shows how these elementary pieces of architecture simultaneously found the city. Our diagram is the diagram of both a hut and a city. We have already noticed the considerable overlapping of the place of gathering and the dwelling. While Vitruvius establishes the primacy of gathering as a precondition for the architecture of the individual hut, it is equally important to recognize the reciprocity between these two, a reciprocity that is visible in the diagram. It is not always a matter of unequivocal public and private activities becoming segregated, distinguished, and protected by assignment to different locations. Rather, there are two independent paradigms that can operate separately or in conjunction to describe a potentially complex and ambiguous pattern of relationships. On one hand, the dwelling serves along with the rest of the political program to help complete this public place, becoming a part of the larger urban structure. In doing so it relinquishes a degree of its privacy in order to take on properties of the public. This need not be considered a loss, but an acknowledgment of the importance of activities and values that are central to domestic life yet must figure as well in the larger political life of community. On the other hand, this dwelling is imagined as being the city itself; a microcosm, subject to the same principles.[17] The manner in which these competing paradigms are accommodated and represented tells much about the political and cultural life of a gathering of people. The resultant architectural structure will be complex or simple relative to the decisions that people agree upon.

The Upright Figure and the Starry Firmament

With this idea of the diagram it will be possible to extract a general understanding of the cultural role of architecture from this mythic origin. As the ability to describe this role also depends on an elucidation of the mental process through which our imagined humans arrive at an understanding of the world, we must return to the moment when Vitruvius offers his most profound distinction between human beings and the other animals. Here, "gifted beyond the other animals in not being obliged to walk with faces to the ground, but upright, and gazing upon the splendor of the starry firmament," these human beings are given a purpose for their existence. While Vitruvius has claimed for his humans many instrumental advantages, these serve only to qualify them as more proficient animals. But the mention of the upright human figure with its elevation over other animals secured by its gazing on the splendor of the starry firmament is an entirely different matter. In an upright position, human beings achieve uniqueness in inquiring about the surrounding world and interpreting its meaning. As a reasoning animal, the human being is able to make a place in the world.

Vitruvius mentions little more than the upright human figure. But this is enough, for with this poetic trope he calls forth the logic of a system of spatial reasoning that is an implicit consequence of the vertical condition. With this spatial reasoning, humans orient their existence in the world and are able to make architecture. The parallel between the origins of speech and the origins of architecture seems more profound.

The making of words is the product of the human being's capacity to make articulate sounds to the degree that some complexity of differentiation is necessary. But this structural capacity alone could never account for the rich diversity of speech that we have come to expect in even the most rudimentary forms of civilization, especially if it were only to be used to serve the fundamental needs of survival. Clearly a purpose is needed that derives from the condition of being human.[18] Vitruvius supplies this first by calling attention to the personal pleasure derived from this primitive wordplay. He then discusses the more substantial and lasting pleasures that accrue as the individual connects to and becomes part of the collective through the initiation of speech and public discourse.[19] Speech, then, has a political intention. It is through speech that the collective works out what it means to live the good life together.[20] Architecture locates this collective in the world.

Vitruvius shows the upright figure inquiring after the splendor of the starry firmament. A connection is implied. Just as the word blossomed into speech as the individual connected to the plurality, so architecture begins when the spatially dislocated individuals of the forest gather to establish a fixed place in the world. The inquiring gaze is the first instance of people's self-consciousness concerning their place in the world.[21] Although they are offered no more than the visible evidence of the skies, they are able to bring to this unmediated sensual experience a conceptual framework that makes the sky intelligible. The skies now become the starry firmament, a symbolic construct that allows inquisitive humans to consider their own position within it. It is the knowledge gained from this act of orientation that provides stability for the foundation of human settlement.[22]

While this knowledge is important, the process through which it is acquired becomes equally important. In order for the idea of the starry firmament to remain vital it must be subject to the fresh speculative gaze of each upright person. In this way its paradigmatic structure is repeatedly reinvented out of the circumstances of each individual life. This process of individual reinvention also insures that the world will have particular meaning for each individual.

Considered as a starry firmament, the sky acquires substantial attributes. This is not a random arrangement of stars in a nebulous sky, but, as the word *firmament* conveys, the vault or arch of the heavens. The heavens, characterized in this way, possess the orderly and systematic structure of a cosmos. Moreover, this structure has its counterpart in the orderly system that underlies the building of the first dwelling.

The upright figure is an important part of this orderly system, in which all of these imputed structures originate. The vertical stance that distinguishes human from animal is a poetic trope, serving to involve both the sensual and the mental apparatus by which order is imparted to and derived from an alien world. Verticality offers a person the most reliable and direct orientational structure by which the world can be interpreted. In contrast to a crawling position, with its horizontal connection to the ground as its only axis of orientation, in the vertical stance all directions of the world (up, down, front, back, left, and right) emanate from a single point as it becomes the center of existence.

This center becomes not only the reference by which the external world is measured and given order, but also the point of reference through which to discover the order inherent in the external world.[23] Even these early observations of the starry firmament would have noted the predictable temporal and spatial pattern of the sun's rising and setting and made use of it to structure human life. Vitruvius has already accounted for the city's location and layout as a response to the actual and imputed qualities of the sun and the winds. Finally, the pull of the earth's gravity, although unknown in a modern scientific sense, was a constant presence that not only affected mobility but forcefully impinged on any building program conceived by speculative upright individuals.

The Task of Architecture

This short narrative by Vitruvius, seemingly as simplistic as a cartoon, can provide a surprisingly rich account of a crucial role for architecture in a continuing process of foundation and renewal of culture. Vitruvius has shown how the condition of individual isolation and dislocation gives way to the pleasures of speech in a fixed place of the human being's own design. These are the preconditions for the unfolding of civilization. The constructed manifestation of this unfolding is an architecture that directly and metaphorically connects the self to the world. Beyond the necessity of survival, this architecture seeks to explain the complex nature of an evolving reciprocal relationship entered into with the hope of securing for the self an existence of lasting value.

This is an architecture unquestionably normative, yet nothing needs to be prescribed. It is grounded in the unchanging fundamental structures of human action and the relatively stable projections of the structure of the cosmos. At the same time, this architecture recognizes and embodies the egotism and boundless inquisitiveness that are such remarkable qualities of the human mind, encouraging an exploration of the limits of knowledge and action. Furthermore, as the constant raising of standards challenges what has been held dear, this architecture assumes that the resulting anxieties are shared amongst the polity and are to be worked out in the public realm. Architecture, for Vitruvius, is an optimistic undertaking that presumes that the shortcomings that are always a part of the present are worth attending to. Finally, architecture is demonstrated to be coterminous with life itself. Architecture does not construct an image of something other than itself; architecture is the making of the human understanding of the world. The places that result enlarge the existence of each individual and help to situate the competing beliefs and aspirations of their disparate participants in a larger and more significant structure.

Of course Vitruvius never described this world. Had he done so, we would have been robbed of the experience of participating in this remarkable story and would have had little incentive to invent our own.

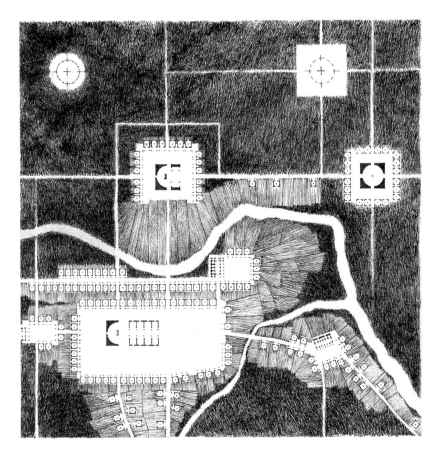

"And so, as they kept coming together in greater numbers into one place, finding them-selves naturally gifted beyond the other animals in not being obliged to walk with faces to the ground, but upright, and gazing upon the splendor of the starry firmament . . . they began in that first assembly to construct shelters." *Drawing by Celia Liu.*

2

Paradigmatic Structures

Architecture holds authority for a culture to the degree that it provides evidence of an ordered world. This evidence of order provides the reliable and predictable grounding necessary for human action to unfold within this world.[1] The order that architecture must establish is a public order, yet accessible to each individual. This is not the world of the solitary individual in the forest, described by Vitruvius as incapable of making architecture until joined with others in the clearing: architecture is derived as a consequence of the initiation of discourse enabled by the gathering. Here also, the nascent political body determines the structure of institutions that will endure beyond each individual life and will ultimately shape the relationships among these people and between them and the earth.

The idea of this first gathering carries an almost unquestionable weight as an exemplar precisely because something was inaugurated here that has persisted. The almost tautological nature of any inauguration allows it to transcend the empirical link between phenomena and form that is the basis of modern science and to a lesser degree of history. Therefore the perennial objective of the treatise writer or theoretician has been to establish an architecture whose authority has been sanctioned by a first cause.

But what exactly do we mean by a beginning? Taken literally, the term is problematic. Any literal first object will be unable to sustain much interest beyond the anecdotal; it could only be a product of a specific response to a particular time and place, and will lack the capacity for generalization and abstraction necessary to generate transferable principles.[2] This archaeological approach also raises a more serious objection: the methods and values of archaeology could never let the claim of a first object stand. Any artifact, no matter how early, must follow from the displacement of something even more primal; the archaeologist's inquiry into beginnings can never, by definition, come to a point of rest. Either the project is rendered futile by an incessant skepticism, or it must contemplate a prior state of absolute nothingness, a consideration that brings little reward.[3] The search for ultimate causes inevitably leads to the unanswerable and frustrates rational discourse.

Christianity deals with this problem rather elegantly by having the *word* already present at the beginning.[4] In this way, the beginning coexists with the conceptual structure of a language that can make this beginning intelligible to its first inhabitants. It is the consequent naming of things, made possible by the word's presence, that we recognize as the first step in a process of giving structure and permanence to the unmediated world of sense impressions. This is the first action of people construing the world.

But was this word actually present at the beginning? As we do not have archaeological evidence, it might be more useful to view the linguistic structure invoked in the fourth gospel as that of an inventive return to an ahistorical origin. With this view we immediately shift attention away from the object and matters of historical record and toward the intentions that would have initiated such a return. The idea of origin, unlike that of beginning, is latent with purpose and intent rather than existing as historical fact.[5] The human condition at this point of origin becomes a worthy object of inquiry when it is less the outcome of an ad hoc causality reacting to the contingencies of time and place, and more the consequence of a purposive intentionality.

A return to origins completely reframes the search for authority, since any return or revisit must necessarily upset the linear continuity that is the basis of historical causality.[6] As this continuity is interrupted, it is confronted by the repeated and discontinuous intentionality that is implicated in beginning again.[7]

To revisit something establishes a relationship with it: the object begins a new life as it is rediscovered or refounded, taking its place as an active participant in the present rather than something remote and historically disengaged. In the same way that we project the vault of the heavens onto our view of a random pattern of stars and planets, we bring preconceived ideas to a revisiting of origins. In the Vitruvian story, then, Vitruvius himself invests a beginning with the intentionality needed to elevate it to the status of mythical origin. To return to an origin or to begin again is clearly not an archaeological project, but an undertaking that seeks to reveal the intentions that must be the basis for human action.

If this effort is to be worthwhile, one must be willing to believe that these fundamental intentions will remain relatively constant, so that the discoveries made in the return can retain validity for an extended period of time, even when subjected to the expected challenges of historical and generational circumstances. Architectural principles derived from such fundamental intentions, conceived to be valid at any time or place, can thus be distinguished from historically contingent rules and exclusions. Architecture, in providing shelter, reveals the human world through this grounding.[8]

The world that so interests us here is not the world of our senses but rather a construct of the mind. Although the raw facts of this world come to us through our senses, it is only after these have been situated within a preexistent paradigmatic structure that they take hold in the imagination. Vitruvius's primitive being looked at the sky and recognized the starry firmament not because it existed as a fixed entity, complete and independent of its observer, but because its unfamiliar structure was just suggestive enough that a known structure might be projected onto it.[9] In this moment the sensual experience of the sky could be given the necessary degree of order to fit into the human world that was being construed.

It is not greatly important whether any particular primitive person actually viewed the sky in this way. The paradigms revealed in Vitruvius's text tell us what he considered necessary to make the world through architecture; they achieve his purpose only if one assumes that they transcend the historical and exist for all. The anonymous stargazer in Vitruvius's tale could just as well be one of us.

The human condition is characterized by its reliance on paradigms.[10] The paradigm, in its most simple sense, is an example or a pattern. This example becomes archetypal as it is invested with the authority of a first cause or instance. We need permanent patterns to give shape to the ephemeral quality of life and action. Thought and consequently action can only take place as a measured response to a structure that is already present in some form. While human cognition operates through paradigms, these originate as independent constructs of the mind rather than as instrumental responses to an external world. Rather than explaining conditions intrinsic to the external world, they act as an index of human intention toward this world.[11]

As a product of human intellection, the paradigm serves as a means for the human being to understand and act in the world. But action, unlike behavior, is never a neutral activity; it is always accompanied by purpose. Likewise the paradigm must be understood as part of a larger critical apparatus. If it were to faithfully replicate something that already exists, little would have been accomplished beyond reproducing the contingent and historical facts of a particular moment. The paradigm has a more ambitious intention, and must be distinguished from the copy. Because of the required verisimilitude, the copy becomes so attached to the object it emulates that any intervention needed for this replication to act critically would compromise the patterns by which the original is recognized. A "critical" copy could only register in the imagination as both formally and intellectually defective. The copy is therefore stranded in an intellectual space where by definition it will always be found inferior to what it imitates, yet be denied the possibility of transformation that might give it a more compelling and autonomous existence. The copy serves only as a substitute for an external reality and in no way advances an understanding of the human being's world. Without an understanding of the world, the human being is unable to be at home within it.[12]

In this context the problem faced by the human being but not the animal is a consequence of our awareness of being placed in a world that we have not designed. Having an innate capacity to construe the world, the human intellect will inevitably find some degree of discordance or discontinuity between the understood world and that which is beyond it. It is precisely in the space created by this discontinuity that the paradigm takes shape as a construct of critical reconciliation or judgment. It is by means of the paradigm that the world out there, a world that it is our particularly human fate to be received into, is reconstituted as the world we might have willed.[13]

As an instrument of critical action, the paradigm will further distinguish itself from the copy. While the latter will tend toward the object of its emulation, ultimately being scarcely distinguished from this, the paradigm moves in the exact opposite direction. The paradigm requires a distance from its object in order to take a stand toward it. The paradigm becomes complex precisely due to the complexity of its relationship to this object. The object or event to which the paradigm is directed must be sufficiently recognizable within the paradigm itself that subsequent interpretation and criticism of the object can be understood. And yet the paradigm must be disengaged from its object so that its own synthetic structure can achieve the degree of coherence that makes it believable. Thus the paradigm, which might begin its life with an almost archetypal simplicity, assumes complexity commensurate with its task of bringing order and understanding to the complex and often contrary condition of being human.[14]

The degree to which any paradigm can remain valid is directly related to its continuing ability to offer a cogent account of the world. When there is doubt, this is usually a consequence of some external disturbance. Either the observable phenomena of the external world fail to correspond to the idea one holds them to, or else the mind itself moves outside the paradigm and from this critical distance discovers some internal incongruity.[15] Irrespective of the cause, the result will be the same: the structure of the paradigm will undergo reconfiguration or transformation. But again, the world that has been constituted through this structure is a product of intellection. As the paradigm draws away from the contingent demands of its object and becomes an abstraction, it is now ruled by the same expectations of structural consistency and coherence as would apply to any mental construct. A reconfiguration therefore, including total replacement, must be guided by the logic of this structure.[16]

It is important to recognize that a paradigm's existence is more dependent on prior paradigms than a response to external actuality. As we construe our world, we first see it through existing paradigms; we may transform or even replace these with other more appropriate models, but we rarely build directly on the raw facts of nature.[17] Pondering this, we might feel anxiety at the apparent loss of creative potential for the human being, who seems to do little more than rework what is already known; or we might feel relief that the daunting task of inventing a world is not one to be faced alone. People have always engaged in this activity. When the task occasionally appears futile, our invisible coworkers offer a certain companionship.[18]

But it would be a misreading of the paradigmatic to think it uninvolved in creative matters. Rather, it is unlikely that any sophistication would be possible without the benefit of some existing structure by which one's thoughts and actions relative to the world could be measured and therefore judged. It is relevant to point out here that the word *invention* has etymological roots in "a coming upon, a discovering or a revealing of something."[19] Implicit is the obvious necessity for that "something" to exist already in some state. Creativity and invention therefore involve the recognition that unexpected potential always exists within something thought to be known.[20] The task of architecture is to reveal these possibilities: truly inventive places have both the security of the known and the potential to accommodate what is yet to be known.

The patterns of everyday life are often so transparent that we are unaware of the structures that shape them, supposing life to be nothing more than a spontaneous response to the world. The child's speech, so wonderfully unselfconscious, nevertheless is impressively coherent because it adheres to an established set of rules. While these might be articulated only by the grammarian, they are implicit in everything the child says.

The most characteristic quality of everyday life is that it appears to us as a pattern of recurring events.[21] It would be difficult to imagine the anxiety that everyday life would present if we were unable to recognize these patterns; we would be incessantly required to invent stopgap measures to avoid disaster. Fortunately, the paradigm provides the means by which recognition is possible. The complementary ability to discern the special from the recurring is equally important. Without the acknowledged structure of the everyday, the exception that rises out of this—the special—would have no place and would be unrecognizable. This certainly would be the ultimate loss of meaning. The paradigm, therefore, by establishing the means by which one can measure the correspondence between a thought or action and some prior datum, establishes the constraint that is the basis for any creative freedom. Acting within this creative freedom made possible by paradigmatic structures, we assume responsibility for making the world.

How is it that the paradigm, a pattern held in common by a culture, can be responsive to the creative will of an individual? Paradigms are not monolithic cultural dinosaurs but are multifarious constructs, offering particular points of access to particular individuals. As a polity is comprised of many individual citizens, a paradigm must be capable of supporting myriad mental meanderings between abstract, ahistorical origins and the unique history of a particular individual. An architectural expression of the paradigm attains its most profound resonances as individual creative possibilities are revealed as potentials within a more simple and overarching public story. The demand for such individual possibilities poses an additional requirement for the paradigm: it must reveal junctions where particular detours could take into account the many possible histories that make up the present.[22]

Etymologically the word *paradigm* includes such meanings as "the set of all inflected forms based on a single stem or theme" and "the display in fixed arrangement of such a set."[23] Thus it already implies a transformative process through which thematic possibilities are explored and represented. The two ideas indicate much about each other. Both paradigm and transformation involve rules that govern their operations, either explicitly or implicitly. In the sense of "paradigm" referred to above, the rigor and the rationality that establishes the structure of a set of grammatical variations are fundamental to its intelligibility. Likewise, the changes in form that are directed by any transformation are expected to have an equal rigor and rationale. We can only analyze speech or writing if we are fully aware of the choices in construction that would have been available and from which a particular configuration under observation could have been deliberately chosen. The multiplicity of differences and the constancy of change are of little interest unless these can be understood as purposeful.

Meaning, in its most abstract sense, is made possible by relationships. We compare and contrast things to one another or to preexisting conditions by means of structures that possess a hierarchy whose rationale is understood and transferable, such as metaphor, analogy, or transformation.[24] However, for meaning to be extracted from some artifact, these valuative structures must be recoverable. Metaphor or analogy not only convey meaning but also can be isolated as structures possessing a degree of independence. Operating in the manner of these linguistic structures, the paradigm similarly demands nothing less than this transferability, recoverability, and independence.

The object of all this attention, the paradigm, is by now becoming considerably encumbered by the complexity and multiplicity of its task. It might help to summarize some of this. First, it needs to be comprehended as a recognizable entity in its own right, while at the same time being transparent to the transformational structures that are implicated or encoded within it. This will demand some trace of the hypothetical reconstitution of the archetypal structure, as well as the embedded notation that records the transformation from this hypothetical origin to its present state. In architecture, I might mention the Greek temple, an artifact constructed of stone as testament to the permanence and stability of a political idea of how the ancient Greek people inhabited the land. And yet the very means of the temple's development and elaboration reveals the coexistence of the fictive wooden architecture that preceded it (in the verdant past of Greek prehistory), constituting its hypothetical origin. Details of this wooden construction, now executed in stone, become witness to the intellectual journey that must have taken place between the conditions surrounding its origins in a remote past (conditions very much a part of the Vitruvian myth of the first dwelling) and the more easily recognized conditions of the present. Included within this interval is the history of both a culture and an architecture, each contributing to the meaning of this increasingly rich artifact.[25]

Finally, we might see in the paradigm the working of tradition. The paradigm has a structure that is continuously accumulating articulate responses to the received world. As a coherent idea of the world is being construed there is a considerable congruity among the parts that constitute the paradigm, and yet this is by no means a static construct. While it is rare that the fundamental structure of the paradigm might require replacement, it is expected that its particular manifestations will be under constant scrutiny. The paradigm's vitality is relevant only to the extent that it offers a compelling account of the world and one that is filled with the capacity for human action. These are qualifications that apply equally to the working of tradition. The root meaning of tradition shows it to be a form of delivery. It is a handing over, but with the implicit understanding that this is done for the purpose of safety, or the saving of something valuable.[26] It also is a handing down, which carries its own implicit extension of generational continuity. Therefore, this activity of delivery carries with it a critical component similar to that of the paradigm. Both demand judgment to discern the value of what is to be handed over, and both imply the accumulation of codified values rather than the simple substitution of one ephemerality for another.[27] The paradigm, like tradition, exhibits a fundamental complicity between its content and the means by which this is delivered. In fact, tradition could be understood as a conservative component of the transformational aspect of the paradigm, in which the past is viewed critically and adjusted to meet the present. If people rely on the paradigm to provide the permanent patterns that make a stable existence possible as they adjust the future to meet their understanding of the past, then they must also rely on tradition to make certain that these paradigms do not suffer from neglect.[28]

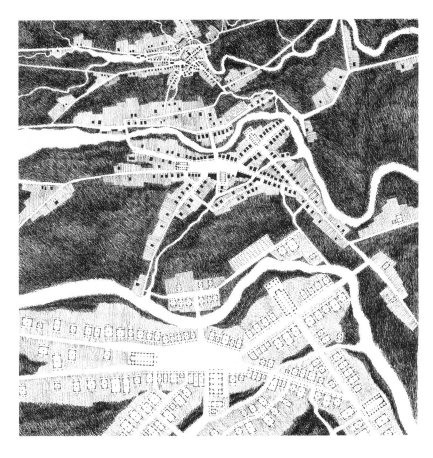

" . . . they next gradually advanced from the construction of buildings to the other arts and sciences, and so passed from a rude and barbarous mode of life to civilization and refinement." *Drawing by Celia Liu.*

3

Action and Representation

One of the remarkable qualities of Vitruvius's mythical reconstitution of the first dwelling is the degree to which the making of architecture is presented as virtually coterminous with existence itself. There is little distinction made between the actions of founding a civilization and the activity of building, and little separation between making and inhabiting architecture. Although an architectural treatise might be expected to emphasize the artifact, Vitruvius seems equally interested in actions of his protagonists that are fundamental to the larger enterprise of dwelling.

Action begins with observing the skies and projecting the structure of a vault onto this sight, as the first sheltering roof for the humans. When the human being connects to the sky and the universe in this way, a world is made present.[1] It is at the center of this world that the human being constructs a dwelling. The subsequent development of this dwelling is described as a process of elaboration through imitation. What so distinguishes this imitative process of making is its location within the public realm as a form of public performance, the purpose of which is the illumination of the idea of dwelling. The primary consequence of this public activity is not an artifact, fixed and imageable, but rather the idea of dwelling: an evolving set of principles that enable the production of "better and better kinds of huts as time went on." Thus the patterns of an ordered existence that are at the foundation of this now purposeful human settlement, patterns that derive their authority from their capacity to give tangible structure to the world, coincide with the structures fundamental to dwelling. The human is constantly engaged in the public performance of gathering together, dwelling, and ultimately building.

The world thus made present is a construed world, a product of human intellection. Although constituted from the observable facts of a natural world by people aware of their history, it must draw away from both nature and history, allowing its own structure to take these contingent conditions into account while offering a more compelling sense of order than they are capable of.[2] The metaphor of the vaulted heavens shows how we select and assemble the visual facts of the sky into the understandable image of a roof, thereby transforming the otherwise vast and nebulous space into a finite closure for our place on earth. But this construed world offers only fleeting stability, as it is continuously in a state of becoming or unfolding in response to evolving human thought and action.

Paradoxically, it is precisely this quality of being open or vulnerable that endows the human's world with authority. This is an authority that is legitimized by its continuing capacity to order the predictable moments of passage that define an individual's life. Thus ordered, the world opens to the inquiry and even to the intervention of human will. Understanding rarely comes in the absence of action. The making of an artifact or an idea is always accompanied by a significant degree of revelation or discovery, far surpassing that of the more passive reception of information. Therefore, the most profound understanding of our world is possible only when we might have invented—or reinvented—that world.[3] This is the task of the architect. It is a task carried out in public, as it demands an audience that is equally engaged in the performance.

Architecture therefore represents the world so that it can make a stable place for people within this world. But what exactly does one mean by representing the world? This is not an easy term. In fact, representation might at first appear to be in conflict with an architecture that engages its public. Much of the difficulty results from the inherent ambiguity of the word itself, with usages that initially appear to be contradictory.[4]

To represent means to make present or to bring into presence. What is made present becomes a tangible reality, an immediate part of human experience. This meaning suggests the revealing of some quality or value that although always in front of us has remained obscured until this point. What is represented, then, is nothing other than itself. If architecture represents the world, then this world must now in some way be present within architecture itself. In other words, the direct physical and sensory experience of relationships within architecture parallel and at critical moments engage those of the larger world. Representation as "making present" seems to be particularly suited to architecture, as architecture differs from other forms of artistic activity in the degree that it directly engages an audience already actively involved in the world. This idea of representation appropriately expands beyond the more passive reception of singular, unambiguous, and conventional meanings carried through signs.[5]

Architecture is not a substitute for something that can never be present—a fate accruing to most artifacts when under the influence of a wistful nostalgia.[6] This surrogate status, however, is exactly the role delegated to architecture under the more common definition of representation as "a replacement or substitute." Implicit in any substitution is an absence that can at best be partially filled by a replacement. Moreover, as the substitute takes the place of what could not be present, its own integrity is compromised in order for it to assume characteristics not necessarily intrinsic to its own makeup, for which it is likely to be materially or intellectually ill equipped.[7] Still, architecture as "replacement or substitute" plays a valuable role under a particular circumstance. This more literal form of representation, whose dependence on convention is so strong, serves well when a very coherent culture is in agreement about the meanings of these conventions.[8]

A third meaning of representation refers to the typical: "to represent" is to typify a class of objects or ideas. This meaning has direct bearing on the making of architecture. Typicality implies that particular entities share at least a minimum of sameness; this sharing is less the result of properties inherent within them and more the product of an extrinsic hypothesis that suggests relationships among pieces of the world. To represent its class, the typical must not be so unique that it can do no more than represent itself, and therefore revert to the particular. We must be able to consider its properties in differing combinations as also fundamental to the makeup of other, not quite similar entities. The typical is one of the products of synthetic thought. In looking for the typical, we assume that what we find in the world will have sufficient integrity of structure that it can satisfy whatever particular need brought it into existence, yet may be able to participate in the forming of larger and more comprehensive structures. In this search, pieces or particulars take on meaning not from their ability to remain distinct from all that surrounds them, but from their differing ability to reveal something fundamentally similar. This possibility alone can both provoke and guide the coming together of a collection of apparently unrelated things to form a coherent world.

Of interest is the considerable overlap between this reference to the typical and the first meaning of "representation" as "the making present of something." In fact, it is from the conjunction of these two meanings that the operations and values of representation become clear. We can imagine the particular, as it is revealed or brought into presence, gaining authority by being rescued from contingency and elevated to the typical. The identification of the typical is part of a process of abstraction that connects the particular to a more general category.[9] In fact, it is at the point of identification of the typical that this process, moving from artifact to idea, intersects a complementary process moving in the opposite direction: the process that transforms the paradigms of placemaking into concrete architectural manifestations.

Diagrammatically one might imagine this as the meeting of two axes. On one axis would be deployed the stages through which something tangible and apparently unique (the particular) is gradually divested of its unique properties on the way to becoming a general statement of typicality. It should be possible to locate the point along this axis where properties of the particular are described in such a general way that they can be seen as also intrinsic to other examples. Through a process of abstraction, that is, it should be possible to determine the exact degree to which it is necessary to draw away from the particular in order to reach a point of congruence with other pieces of the world, noting precisely what specificities have been taken away, and the means by which this has been accomplished. The consequence of this process is the location of a particular instance of something within a larger and hierarchically differentiated framework of entities with similar qualities. Now the special attributes that make the particular unique and compelling can be incorporated within this framework, giving it a more stable place, while enlarging the meaning of the new synthetic construct. The value of the typical comes from the hypotheses that we must make in order to propose that some thing or some action might be a part of an ever-increasing world of connected pieces. This process, of course, can never be mistaken as neutral. It is yet another means through which human beings take a stand in order to construe the world.[10]

Referring to our diagram, we might imagine a second axis passing through the typical, on which would be arrayed a series of transformations made to one of the fundamental paradigms that direct the human being's inhabitation of the earth. These paradigms, like all paradigms, have no concrete presence and are thus removed from human experience; they can be approached but never fully grasped. Through a process the inverse of that just described for making hypotheses about the typical, it is possible to bring a sufficient degree of specificity to the paradigm. Responding to the contingencies of time and place, the evanescent idea can be embodied within the particular and the concrete and as such can be open to experience. Although this process begins in the indefinite realm of idea, it concludes in very particular places of gathering and dwelling.[11]

It is at the point of conceptual intersection where particular manifestations are made present as typical that the structure of the paradigm is fleetingly revealed before passing into some specific example and becoming obscured again.[12] Here its structure is latent with all the potential unique to the paradigm and yet similarly latent with the multiplicity of potential locations within time and place. The meaning that derives from representation is a consequence of making present the specific judgments that are required to bring about these transformations converging around the typical.[13] The purpose of representation is to give shape to the contingency of existence by means of the paradigmatic structure that is simultaneously constituted and revealed through this process.

The column is an instructive example of how this process of representation works. Most treatises, beginning with Vitruvius's, locate the origin of the column outside of history, at the moment when a mythic ancestor removed a tree from its contingent life within the forest by unloading it of its natural content and thus enabled it to participate in the world of human purpose. This was accomplished either by uprooting it and placing it upside down with roots as a crude and ironic capital (its head) or by allowing it to remain rooted in the ground but stripped (abstracted) of those characteristics that otherwise would cause it to register in the human imagination as merely a tree.[14] An alternate account, also proposed by Vitruvius, locates the column's origin in an exemplary human being from whom were abstracted more general properties that could be made present to the public as a column.[15]

However, for any later builder to return to this moment of origin by using a literal tree or depicting a particular human figure (as was done in the case of the caryatids) would not allow for a distance sufficient for this particular embodiment to be transformed into the typical. One would not have conveyed meaning beyond the functional capacity of the tree to bear loads, and in the case of the human figure there might be the unintended but inevitable anxiety about how long it might remain bearing its load. Moreover, these two literal models, the tree and the human figure, each have such particular meaning that it is difficult to discern anything other than differences between them, leading to the unwarranted conclusion that one of them must be preferable. This is the problem of analytical thinking: the tendency to amplify difference such that our preference will be fully justified.[16] This polarization unfortunately precludes the possibility of meaning being derived equally from several sources. It also limits the ability to compare more abstract ideas of the tree to the human figure and speculate on the far more valuable possibility of their congruence.

Instead, beginning with the common vertical stance shared by tree and human figure and their parallel relationship between ground and sky, one might propose even more significant points of congruence that bring the worlds of nature and the human being together. The column acknowledges the particular meanings that pass through it not by portraying their external form through signs, but by abstracting or condensing their salient characteristics. This requires an act of judgment that itself is recoverable as part of the process now encoded within the column. Since this is a role played by all columns, we are further made aware of how this particular column is indebted to the columns that preceded it. In other words, the column, as a general class of objects, has a history that situates each particular column within a conventional system of meaning. Within these conventions, our column can be compared to others. The precise registration of the degree of similarity or difference confers on this column quite specific associations. Finally, yet most important, there is the idea that is represented in the term "orders." The word itself suggests a role for the column beyond its function as a structural prop. As it is implicated historically in an extensive and systematic way of building, the column makes present a pattern of human order by finding a correspondence between this and the order of nature. As we view this column, now speculating systematically on the encoded information that it makes present, we are aware of ourselves as interpreting beings equipped with quite specific means to see and understand the world.[17]

What I hope is evident in this example is the degree to which meaning is intrinsic to the object yet requires the engagement of an audience or participant to bring this to presence. The discovery thus made present is both predictable and unexpected. The object establishes a probable constellation of meanings and sets certain limits; the discovery is made increasingly present as it takes hold of the human imagination. Representation requires a collaboration between the object and the subject. As one draws away from the object, often by omitting or veiling those characteristics within which reside the greatest degree of expressive specificity, the resultant abstraction enables the missing pieces to be filled in by means of an imaginative reconstitution that brings its own memories, hopes, and aspirations to a receptive architecture. The meaning that is the most real is the one closest to the experiences and memories that define the character of this human subject.[18]

An architecture that tries to prescribe existence can succeed only when the members of its audience are in complete agreement and will remain so for the expected life of its constructs. Since this condition is achievable only under circumstances that most would find intolerable or at best improbable, such an architecture will fail to make present anything of value to most who encounter it. But an architecture that is capable of the continuous renewal of the world as it accepts the critical interpretation of an engaged public will persist as a compelling presence.

For architecture to guarantee a mutual understanding between a building and its public, it needs a degree of intellectual and emotional access that is only afforded by abstraction.[19] It is through the process of abstracting that one establishes a relationship between a particular object, unique to its specific context, and a representation of this object as a part of the more general category of objects familiar in differing ways to the public. I am referring here to generally accepted and etymologically derived usages of the terms "representation" and "abstraction." I find current usages of these terms in art historical discourse problematic. "Representation" is often aligned with the rather recent and specialized term "representational" to refer to an accurate reproduction or copy. Matters are further confounded by the appropriation from the world of art of a usage for "abstraction" that stresses its completely nonreferential intentions. In concert, these usages tend to polarize a relationship that otherwise would clearly be mutually dependent. The outcome of this polarization is that, on one hand, representation is mistaken for the object of its emulation, and, on the other, abstraction becomes an isolated goal detached from any object. This is a false opposition. Abstraction cannot exist in isolation, since it is the very means by which it is possible to represent the object. These terms are more properly seen as complementary. A relationship between representation and abstraction that avoids polarization also reveals a strong structural parallel between abstraction and the several usages of the paradigm, as one can now see these terms exploiting a full range of possibilities while moving between the poles of generalization and particularity.

If we can agree that representation requires distance from the object of its emulation, can we determine the extent of this distance? The response to this inquiry carries consequences. The closer the representation is to its object, the more specific will be the reference, and conversely as one abstracts from this object, the representation becomes more general and universal, increasingly admitting of more possible meanings.[20] As in most things, it may be advisable to avoid the extremes. Abstraction taken too far allows any meaning to pass through it, thus rendering impossible the very idea of meaning. Conversely, a representation that fails to gain significant distance from its object will exclude any additional possibilities of critical interpretation, leaving the representation metaphorically empty. As a representation becomes more abstract and less specific, one puts aside the accumulated layers of meanings that are the outcome of the particular history of the object of representation. The object is therefore rendered available to an increasing audience that might otherwise have been kept away by a lack of knowledge of the specifics of this history. The accumulated layers of meaning are not discarded, however, but are merely less obviously present, contributing to the total impression of the work recognized by all and offering a further depth of understanding to those holding more specialized knowledge.[21] It is the paradigmatic structure that provides the predictable stability that can support these multiple layers, so that any object might be rendered appropriately meaningful to a differentiated public.

The abstraction of the narrative tradition of oral storytelling provides an interesting comparison to architecture in terms of its ability to represent the world.[22] For most of us accustomed to the authority of the written document as a means of communicating information, it is difficult to imagine how compellingly the epic storyteller presented an account of the paradigms necessary for people to deal with each other and the world. Hence we are unaware that a public realm can be established through these stories, as well as a tradition maintained through the process by which they are told.[23]

The epic storyteller or singer is retelling a traditional story. But we must not think of this story in terms of a written narration, since what exists is only a deliberately vague skeleton or outline of events and relationships at once highly condensed yet necessarily generalized. We might even wish to think of it as an abstraction. The mythos, as the Greeks referred to this story, was a paradigmatic structure intended to give order to the circumstances that define a shared existence among people. It was by means of the mythos that death, the failure of crops, and other misfortunes of history might become bearable as these are rescued from an ineluctable fate, not with the expectation of reversing this fate, but rather with the belief that an understanding of the order of things might provide enough of a sense of cause that further action becomes possible.

The mythos is made present as a song through the medium of the performance. Until the narrative is actually sung, that song exists only as a potential story, and conversely when the song is over it ceases to exist. The performance, although originating in the structure of the mythos (and the shared values it implies), becomes an experience unique to the singer as well as to each individual within the audience who witnesses that particular performance. This unique experience, then, is the outcome of the collaboration between the singer and the members of the audience. The mythos remains stable, yet each performance has the capacity to enlarge the idea of the mythos as the song reveals some new understanding within the singer or the audience. The song, which is the performance itself, cannot be transmitted; only elements are transmitted, such as plot, certain episodes, conception of character. Therefore, the performance is capable of assuming some degree of permanence only to the extent that the structure of intentionality erected by this collaboration, and residing in the memories of those present, informs the tradition from which the mythos is born and affects the subsequent actions of people.

As we understand the potential of the oral tradition, we become aware of the limits of representation. We are faced with the paradoxical condition in which the same story, the mythos, is retold countless times yet the permanent trace of its existence (that which can be carried away or transmitted) resides only in one's memory. The apparent remedy for this, the written narrative, can only represent the performance as a substitute, and a necessarily inferior substitute due to its being removed from the direct experience of the performance. It is virtually impossible to capture with the same intensity all of the nuances that result from the interrelationships among the singer, the audience, and most importantly the place. But even more problematic is the consequent closing of the boundaries of the mythos to any further enlargement. As the written account becomes a rival to the song, it can accomplish this only as it attempts to faithfully replicate a particular performance from the point of view of a single individual. Now the written song, originally only one of the many potential manifestations of the mythos resulting from the particular circumstances surrounding the intersection of singer, audience, and place, becomes synonymous with the mythos itself, and the paradigmatic capacity of the mythos to elevate these particular circumstances to the typical is lost as the song is reduced to historical record. But this historical record has status only as one of the many that might have been written—as many as there might have been members in the audience. Unlike the song of the oral tradition, which was understood as holding its allegiance always to the mythos even while it produced transformations in response to the contingencies of time and place, the many historical records register little more than their difference from one another, with each now claiming an impossible authority. Of course, one could see the plots of current novels as mythically derived. The novels then become a performance for a particular generation, and succeed to the extent that they are able to connect with the values and particularities of that audience.

Yet what distinguishes the oral from the written is the authority the mythos gains due to the necessity for public action. The oral tradition requires the assembly of individuals to make an audience. But the relationship between this audience and the singer differs from the theatrical convention that divides the performance into the real and the illusory, with the actor presenting some fiction to an audience whose grasp on reality is believed to be secure. Within the oral tradition, reality resides in the mythos. Although originally in the possession of the singer, the veiled outline of this mythos assumes form and authority only as it responds to the particular needs of an engaged public. As the singer and the audience engage one another in the performance, the audience is prompted to measure its collective history as well as the histories of its individual members and compare these to the timelessness of the mythos.[24] Thus it is the performance that reveals how the constancy and stability of the human condition (the mythos) lends support to and explanation of the contingent, the particular, and the historical while endowing these with human purpose.

It is again worth mention that by intention the mythos never changes, always existing as a paradigm.[25] But rather than reducing the richness and complexity of human existence to something so unambiguously general as a paradigm, it is the performance itself that demands the elaboration, the qualification, and the particularization that both singer and audience bring to the event. Thus the certainty and the stability that support and sustain the possibility of a purposeful human existence are also there to make a place for each individual life.

Vitruvius describes a nearly identical condition when he speculates on the way the first architects went about making, emulating, and judging their architecture. They too did this as public performance: a performance that could be understood and valued by all. The activities of people constructing their world and the rituals and ceremonies of habitation that are enabled and signified by the resultant architecture do not refer to things outside themselves, nor are they substitutes for something unable to be actually present, but are most emphatically a part of the direct experience of participating in making the world.

In looking for specific parallels to the performance of the oral tradition, we might consider the plan to be that aspect of architecture that engages its public in the most direct manner. The plan is the means by which we ground our existence in a specific place while simultaneously connecting this place to all the places that make up the web of human existence. The plan makes present the surface on which we walk, giving measure to the earth through our rhythmic stride. The consequent plane, leveled to aid mobility, frees us from the overwhelming complexity of our natural surroundings yet aligns us to a visible and stable horizon. The rising and setting of the sun gives concrete evidence of where we are oriented relative to the cardinal mapping of the world. The plan determines the boundaries within which our lives unfold. Its structure is a paradigm for the structure of human relationships as it simultaneously divides people and their activities from one another and yet brings these together. The fit between the plan and the structure of relationships it is able to support is loose, offering a considerable latitude of choice as to how it might be inhabited.[26] It is this latitude of choice that enables us to further engage the plan, and it is the hierarchy of the plan's structure that weights our choices, such that any particular choice will disclose the values by which we make decisions about our world. These structures are made present and are given authority through our participation in this process of self-judgment.

The plan is, however, an abstraction. Although it may be experienced through direct sensory means and as such can be the cause of an immediate physical reaction, it is equally effective in representing the potential for action that might be enabled by its structure. Just as the place of performance where the singer creates the song has the mnemonic capacity to aid the recall of the audience even after the performance has ended, so the plan need not literally have its surface walked on to have its import understood.[27]

Yet when architecture becomes disengaged from the public realm—either through its becoming the private voice of one person or because of an uninterested public—and consequently becomes estranged from the actions of people securing their place in the world, then the making and the representing of architecture become separate and disconnected activities. Representation now becomes a substitution or replacement for something not present, and architecture is thought of more as a thing—complete in itself—and therefore closed to further intervention and disclosure. As such, building begins to assume more the characteristics of written narration and, indeed, is thought of as a form of legible text, capable of being read much as if it were a book.

As a metaphor, this analogy to a book has a certain utility, especially in reference to the significant structural similarities between the two, but its overextension is problematic. The most immediate consequence is the reduction of meaning inherent to architecture, as its content is emptied of any purpose beyond the ability to communicate and architecture itself becomes transparent to the necessarily extrinsic meanings that pass through it, much the way the artifactuality of the book disappears relative to its content.[28]

If, for the sake of argument, we accept this role for architecture, then we must be satisfied with the diminished expressive capacity that results when content that has been produced within one medium is transferred to another without the transformations that are essential to the processes of representation and abstraction. One has only to compare a musical performance with its literary description to realize that although each has its purpose these are not mutually transferable with any degree of success. Architecture's silence stands to remind us that when asked to speak, buildings have only had recourse to words, relief sculpture, or other media that have been literally inscribed on or affixed to their surfaces.[29]

My point here is not to limit the means of representation available to architecture. Instead, in reiterating that the fundamental purpose of architecture is to construe the world and thus orient the actions of people, I want to establish that this is a task that is inextricably bound up with the representational means belonging to the compositional paradigms that are the basis of architecture.[30] The need to borrow from or to substitute the representational apparatus of other disciplines may indicate that architecture is being asked to fulfill a role outside its most fundamental purpose. It most definitely does not come from any deficiency in architecture's own representational capabilities.

"Then, taking courage and looking forward from the standpoint of higher ideas born of the multiplication of the arts, they gave up huts and began to build houses with foundations, having brick or stone walls, and roofs of timber and tiles; next, observation and application led them from fluctuating and indefinite conceptions to definite rules of symmetry." *Drawing by Celia Liu.*

4

The Structure of Paradigms

Meaning derives from relationships. We compare known and unknown things with one another and also with logical structures that
might be external to them. The purpose is not merely to distinguish
things from one another, but to establish hierarchies that allow the
attribution of value to the things that make up the world. While some
of these hierarchical structures represent the accumulated conventions
of a particular place and time, most of them derive from the innate
perceptual and conceptual structures through which the human being
brings order to the world. Hence, although outside of convention,
these structures are not outside the realm of human understanding
and action.[1]

Unfortunately, modern scientific thought has tended to systematically erase any anthropological reference from its description of the
world. Scientific description is unable to take hold of the imagination
in the same way as the structures we erect out of the fundamental intellectual and sensory apparatus that all human beings hold in common.
The latter are notable because of the immediacy with which they are
able to direct our lives. Vitruvius's early architects are thus able to con-
fidently construe their world and situate their dwellings at its center.
The center of their world is the center of a complex web of relationships that defines their existence and connects this to all they know of
the universe. The coherence of this world is the intentional consequence of a synthetic outlook that always strives for unity.[2] Its structure

is not dependent on the physical sciences for external topographical verification, since the analytical certainty that science promises through its quantification of the pieces of the universe often fails to adequately and imaginatively represent a reality in which human beings can act.

As we have seen, this world begins to assume structure with the actions of the upright figure gazing on the starry firmament. This first act of orientation is able to locate a place of human settlement at a topological center of the world. It proceeds, with little additional assistance, to establish the boundaries and ultimately to define the hierarchies by which the group's actions become significant to themselves.

But how different from us are the stargazers that Vitruvius describes? Is our world different from the world of those times? Human eyes still see the same rising and setting sun; the same mental structure still gives order to the perception of the sun's movement, enabling this to become a predictable part of a purposefully construed world. Our world may differ in the vast amount of information that so casually is made available, yet this too must be given order as we render the judgments demanded for this information to pass into the realm of knowledge, and therefore to affect action. It is the constancy of the structure by which the mind brings order to the world that endows our world with forms comparable to those Vitruvius describes. Perhaps, as we have become distracted by apparent difference, we have forgotten how much remains the same. It is with this thought that I wish to reintroduce the human figure and the relationships it persistently enters into with the world. These are the basis for the paradigms fundamental to architectural composition.

Vitruvius bestows on the human being its advantage over the other animals through a poetic trope that establishes the conditions and the means by which this human being will make a place in the world. Human beings are described as "not being obliged to walk with faces to the ground, but upright, and gazing upon the splendor of the starry firmament." A distinction has been made between instinctual behavior that functions solely to guarantee the survival of the species and purposeful action that seeks, through the legitimizing forum of public performance, to perpetuate the more fragile accomplishments of people beyond their short mortal existence. For the human being, this is the means to counteract the seeming futility of individual life. The analysis of this purposeful action and the structures it produces offers much greater reward than the analysis of the instinctual patterns of behavior over which we have little control.

The human being also is an animal, and human behavior is likewise driven to satisfy basic needs in order to survive. However, unlike the other animals, which suffer little anxiety about choices they will never have to make, the human being's need to understand the self and the world this self inhabits causes it to ask other types of questions.[3] The choices that these questions make available are both liberating and profoundly troubling. The animal wants only to know how to most efficiently satisfy an immediate craving, but the human being needs to know why.[4] Humans, unlike animals, are constantly faced with decisions that put the justifications they contrive for a meaningful existence in conflict with the behavior that insures their survival. The constant tension that results is fundamental to our understanding of the places people make and within which their lives unfold.

The structure and meaning of these places reveal a significant paradox, directly attributable to the dual nature of the human condition. The most fundamental level of security for the human being is achieved simply by maintaining physical separation from the natural world. In the Vitruvian story this is accomplished by means of the fire. But physical protection from nature, attained by keeping the animals at bay and keeping the human being warm, is clearly not a sufficiently compelling end for human existence. People need protection that is of their own devising and addresses their own purposes and intentions.[5] This must be more than a reaction to the contingencies of nature, and it must be effected by means that suit human purpose. The human being accepts the separation offered by the fire only to the degree that its fleeting stability provides an initial respite from nature that allows a stand to be taken, situating human existence within the world.

This is a place constituted and given order by paradigms that derive from the structure of the human being and represent an existence unique to human purpose. Yet the separation from the natural world can only be provisional. Its certainty will soon give way to ambiguity as people inquire and extend themselves into an ever larger world. This is the significance of the purposeful upward gaze of the human being, metaphorically connecting to the splendors of the starry firmament.

Our need to define human existence as distinct from nature coincides with the realization of the costs of this estrangement. The means by which people establish their separation from nature, therefore, should not be taken as antinomies incapable of resolution.[6] The example of the fire is instructive. Its origin is in the natural world, and people are terrified by it and need to escape from its furious flames. Yet the fire is the agent by which these same people are protected from the natural world, enabling them to construe a world of their own. Its heat and light initially provide the direct stimulus for public assembly. Soon, however, this deliberative assembly itself becomes the purposeful action that distinguishes people from their surrounding and the fire assumes the totemic role of hearth, marking both the place and the occasion of this gathering. Finally this passes into language as a metaphor for the stability of domesticity. Architecture becomes necessarily complex and multivalent as it represents a reality that manifests itself in such contradictory ways.[7]

Center

It is precisely at the moment that we stand up to nature and offer a human account of the world that the character of the structure that will guide our destiny is determined. This structure begins at a center, defined (either individually or collectively) by the sensory and intellectual act of viewing the world from the fixed point of a particular location.[8] People exist securely within their world because its order begins with themselves and radiates outward. What they know of the world is measured from this place, with the greatest degree of certainty the closest to this center.[9] As the distance from the center increases and its influence diminishes, the domain over which this center must continue to preside needs to be increasingly secure. Its boundaries will demand physical and even metaphysical means of enclosure, for what is beyond can only be the chaos and confusion of a world yet to be known.[10]

The "stand" we take is not merely metaphorical, since it stems from the literal circumstance of the verticality of our stance and the consequent situation of our eyes which directs our gaze forward. The structure that radiates outward from this point is more than the homogeneous and neutral space of a rationalized Cartesian geometry, where all directions are spatial coordinates intentionally emptied of signification. Unlike this, our structure is highly charged and hierarchically differentiated.[11] Beginning at this center, the directions—forward, backward, left, right, and up and down—can be projected onto a ground and sky, endowing these with a paradigmatic structure capable of creating a matrix of related meaningful places.[12] These directions assume significance as a direct consequence of the structural differentiation of the human figure. The strength of this parallel has long been made explicit in language. Humans achieve the verticality that allows their gaze to travel so far only as they resist the relentless pull of the earth's gravity. This seemingly unremarkable but constantly repeated victory is noted in our uses of the words "up" and "down," in which "upward mobility," for instance, is preferable to being "down and out." The frontal plane of our eyes establishes a perpendicular axis extending forward and directing passage along it. Both the implied axis of our forward gaze and the path it projects on the earth give order to our actions. This too is recorded in common usage in the terms "forward" and "backward," which carry unusually strong spatial and linguistic bias. Worth mention is the singularity of this frontal plane, for we certainly would not wish to be thought of as "two-faced." Even the apparently minor asymmetries of the human body promote a distinction between its two sides, with the right having connotations of correct and accurate, while those of the left are suggested by the French equivalent *gauche* or the Italian *sinistra*.[13]

These relationships establish the fundamental connection between humans and the earth.[14] But when we return to the upright figure and the starry firmament, we now need to deal with a more difficult and problematic relationship. The verticality that is made explicit at the center, and which we have traced as a vehicle providing a fixed orientation and point of reference for our actions on the earth, must now connect to realms beyond the earth.[15] The vertical closure inherent in the human figure, with its feet on the ground and its head directing a forward gaze onto the distant horizon, can now be equally understood as a fragment of a more extensive set of connections linking the sky above to the underground below. At this point the full potential of the center is realized.[16] Here our path on the earth, which defines the history of our entire profane existence, intersects the vertical axis that represents the full cycle of our lives from birth to death.[17] Actions that are situated within this vertical structure take on profoundly different meanings. Underground and sky, cellar and attic, foundation and roof are structured about the human center, yet due to projected and inherent values are related in only the most asymmetrical of constructs.[18]

Boundary

The center locates one in the world, but the center cannot exist without an edge or boundary. Without a limit to its authority, the center cannot be a center to anything particular. The relationship between the center and its edge is thus more complicated and reciprocal than it would first appear. It is easy to recognize the authority that can be invested in the center, yet the edge is also significant: the edge determines exactly what is inside, and therefore it determines what is most reliably known.[19]

To a considerable degree this opposition of inside and outside is a construed rather than a received phenomenon.[20] The human being has eternally sought the protection and security of an inside safe from both the real and imagined dangers of the outside.[21] The complementary relationship of inside and outside is thus constituted as much from the need to secure and control this opposition as from a response to the immediacy of contingent danger.[22] The boundary is an a priori structure whose presence itself brings these distinctions into being.[23] The boundary further participates by establishing the conditions under which the inside and the outside will be allowed to engage one another. This edge therefore is a rather paradoxical construct, both separating and connecting the two realms it has revealed.[24] This is as much a critical action as it is a protective one, since it is through the device of the edge that it is possible to understand and give value to the differences between the world that is ours and the indeterminate and unknown expanse beyond.

The edge, then, cannot be defined geometrically as a line with no breadth, since it must have sufficient material and intellectual dimension to appropriately bound the two very different and necessarily discrete conditions of inside and outside.[25] As the edge responds differ-ently to the situation on either side, it becomes more articulate. It must now have two distinct and independent sides. These two sides occasion yet another side, and that is the in-side or space between. In other words, the edge itself has an interior, and it follows that this too might be able to be inhabited.[26] But existence within the edge is precarious. Within the edge humans are without status in either world; although separated from the public realm of gathering and discourse, they are equally estranged from the comforts of dwelling that define private life. Existence within this liminal zone therefore is best thought of as very temporary. However, this anxious condition is not without poten-tial reward, as people in this situation must come to their own conclu-sions about these opposing worlds and chart their own course for dealing with their separation or connection when they return to the security of either side.

The distinction people make between their known world and the outside becomes manifest in several ways. In the Vitruvian tale, the trees that will eventually become the edge to a clearing initially exist as part of an undifferentiated natural world. They become construed as part of the human being's world only when the latter makes a dis-tinction between solitary life in the forest prior to the fire and the pur-poseful actions of political people gathered in deliberative assembly around the dying embers.[27] The fire becomes their center, and its authority extends over an inside defined by the edge of the forest. Now this edge is constituted as a boundary through the purposive actions of these people. The edge might equally have been made from other found natural conditions. Landforms such as mountain ranges, hills, and valleys all have physical characteristics that allow them to be en-dowed with human structure, and therefore to be brought into the realm of human purpose.[28]

Inside and outside are further distinguished in terms of changes in height made to the ground plane. As the ground plane is demarcated, elevated, and given a new order, it is distinguished from its less regular surrounding. Thus human beings achieve a sense of security by liter-ally removing themselves from the earth, making it possible to easily establish a new order and marking a ground that is closer to their intentions. Yet even this literal disengagement is countered by the implied reattachment that is the result of the view from the eye being extended by its new height to an ever more distant horizon.

The underlying structure of nature and the construed order of the human being are both made present through these actions. The direction of causality, however, is not always certain. When the human being takes advantage of natural conditions within the found landscape, is this because of qualities solely intrinsic to these conditions, or are these conditions found in the first place because they match some paradigm that the human being brings to an otherwise more neutral configuration?[29] If nature is to participate in the human world, or conversely if human beings hope to retain their tenancy within the natural world, then both must engage the boundary as equal players. While in the past this has meant an act of heroic bravery on the part of the human being, perhaps this equality now demands human restraint and humility. Where everything is solely the result of human endeavor, the boundary is lost. The multiplicity of processes and circumstances that comprise the character of the earth must be able to coexist at least equally with the paradigms that the human being projects on the earth. This equality can occur through the human process of abstracting from natural processes and circumstances to conceive and then build the synthetic structures that are a local attempt to subsume both worlds. In this way, the human artifact can respond to the myriad particularities of the received facts of nature while simultaneously marking a particular local transcendence of these, in order to represent a purpose we hope will be universal and enduring.

Entry-Passage

The distinction between an inside and an outside thus grows from the circumstances of the human condition. To be inside, at least metaphorically, is to have the essential knowledge that allows one to be at home in the world. This knowledge begins with the human figure as the primary point of reference; all that is outside is measured against and compared with this figure, so as eventually to make the outside equally known and habitable. The comparison is made possible by the controlled passage by which one departs from and returns to the security of a known place. When Vitruvius's primitive dwellers are first found in their clearing, they have come from the forest but they have not entered a place, since the existence of any place requires a constitutional intent that will only arise later as a consequence of their deliberative assembly around the central focus of the fire. Paradoxically, when they make their first entry, it is *from* the place of the fire as they return to visit the forest. Now, however, the forest is understood as the outside, an outside that is open to further understanding through the extension of the order already established within the clearing. Finally, as they arrive back in the clearing, they return to this place with knowledge of a previously unknown world (the outside) that, when compared and judged relative to what they have known inside, enlarges their understanding both of their world and of themselves.

Entry is constituted when the edge or boundary must be broken to afford direct passage between the inside and the outside. It is here that these opposed worlds are experienced and understood with the greatest intensity, as both are collapsed into the liminal threshold of entry. The entry is the place that makes present the distinction between what is known and what is unknown about the world, and it is here that one begins the interpretation of this relationship in order to attribute purpose to this representation of difference.[30]

Like the boundary, entry is a complex and paradoxical construct. The portal itself, as it comes to us from early foundation ceremonies, was simply that place where the cutting of the protective furrow that initially defined the secure world of the inside was interrupted, the plow being lifted and carried to allow at that one place a literal continuity of the ground between outside and inside.[31] This continuity, however, required special means to protect a distinction now rendered vulnerable in this place. Physical protection is afforded easily by gates, doors, and other movable barriers, but these seem to offer a protection curiously at odds with the uninterrupted boundary provided by the plowed furrow. These physical deterrents are either overscaled to their task or more probably fall short, as more is at stake here than physical security. The problem of entry, then, is a consequence of the need for literal passage across a boundary that establishes a fundamental opposition; any physical opening providing for passage must be countered by a deterrent that maintains the strength of the conceptual opposition. While physical barriers can always be breached, the less material and more metaphysical obstacles associated with entry are violated with greater peril. We have only to note the prohibitions against an unsanctioned marriage that cause the eloping bride to leave her parents' house not through the legitimacy of the entrance, but by the more illicit window and ladder.

The entrance is thus necessarily an ambiguous construct, since it must reconcile the contradictory demands of protection and engagement without compromising either. These conflicting conditions are not set up as opposed and unresolvable antinomies but are defined through multiple and redundant pairings that intentionally overlap, so that no single instance of connection or separation will preclude its inverse from being equally present. The most important pairing, and one that affects everything that follows, is the relationship that is established between the center and the bounding edge of any place. Because of the structural differences between these, there is a considerable redundancy in how each defines this place. Together, as they interact to reinforce as well as counter each other, they become the basis of all further elaboration.

The center is the actual or implicit goal that one is directed to while passing across the edge, and conversely it is from the center that one orients passage into the world beyond this edge. The place of entry, therefore, is both extensive and labyrinthine. It attaches the center to a world beyond that which its boundary makes secure. At the same time, the entry engages the space in this interval as part of the process. Now the division between inside and outside that is literally made at the edge can be countered by the horizontal extension of a path formed to both regulate and represent the actual or implied difficulty of passage that connects the edge to the center. The space along this path, which of course includes both inside and outside, is therefore endowed with purpose. Its structure is the result of the relationships it establishes between the center and what is outside. As passage is made more difficult, the goal becomes more worthy of achievement, and as one moves closer to the goal, the value of this location increases.[32] This somewhat linear progression becomes an armature that allows the actions along it to be measured, compared, and ultimately given value. But each action along the way calls for its own place distinct from and yet attached to all that surrounds it. These places also require thresholds that mediate between a local inside and outside. As part of a more extensive structure, these thresholds replicate relevant aspects of the structure of the larger place and yet are distinguished from this by their transformational response to their local situation. Thus the path and the places this path gives structure to are ordered along the conceptual axis relating the center of settlement, and therefore its purpose, to both the fact and idea of what is outside. It is this relationship that establishes the principal structure of the settlement.

This relationship of the center to the outside also works as a catalyst at the level of the constituent part. The part participates in the structure of the settlement in two fundamental ways. Either it acts as a microcosm of the whole, thus elevating the status of any associated activity, or it exists as a fragment that becomes important as it combines with other fragments to complete the whole.[33] In either case, as the part is transformed with respect to the structure of the whole, the ensuing relationship between the transformed part and the whole will promote a comparison between the two. The part will be understood as reinforcing the structure and the values of the whole, or it might bring additional qualifications to this structure arising from its own particular response to the world.

It should be clear that the path that the human being charts or follows has a more ambitious task than simply transportation between two points.

Two different systems of spatial orientation are in evidence here. The center marks a discrete and fixed point around which the world is concentrated. Its stability is the basis on which one erects the structure of a place. Yet, for this place to engage a larger world in order to make this known and therefore habitable, a horizontal extension is required which is the primary structure of the path. Thus it is through the complementary construct of concentration and extension, or place and path, that the world is given an order that can support a meaningful existence. Passage along its actual or implied length engages the human being in the constitution of the world. This project presents such challenges that the relationships enumerated above are only the foundation upon which additional transformations and elaborations will act to represent a rich and varied account of human purpose.

Geometry

In the introduction to the sixth book, Vitruvius recounts the story of the Socratic philosopher Aristippus who, shipwrecked and cast ashore on the coast of the Rhodians, observed geometrical figures drawn on the land and cried out to his companions: "Let us be of good cheer, for I see the traces of man."[34] Vitruvius uses this tale to illustrate the portability of learning and to demonstrate its greater value than the acquisition of worldly goods when confronting the uncertainty of an unexpected arrival in a foreign setting. What is of interest is that he offers geometry as his example of learning. Although more sophisticated than the mythic first builders, Aristippus and his crew found themselves in circumstances that are roughly parallel. Both were traumatically dislodged from the natural world, and as a result both needed to make a place in a world not yet known to them. The mythic builders construed their world as they compared their new setting to what they knew of themselves and adjusted it accordingly. The later philosopher, however, discovered the traces of purposeful action already extant. This gave him confidence that, although in a land foreign and literally unknown, he had nevertheless arrived at a place he could understand as home. Without the prior knowledge of this new place that presumably could have come from a familiarity with its history, Aristippus relied on the more universally recoverable order that is the consequence of geometrical mapping. This ability, we are led to believe, is not something unique to the philosopher Aristippus but rather an innate part of the conceptual apparatus of every human being.

Geometry means "earth measure."[35] While its practice probably originated in Egypt as a means to measure fields after the periodical flooding of the Nile, its theory and naming were Greek.[36] Its origin seems pragmatic, but its development as a series of postulates with internally consistent proofs gives it a logic so compelling that it has persisted as a datum by which to measure and compare phenomena existing even outside of this logic. The geometrical structures that are the manifestations of these postulates (such as the axis, the right angle, the circle and square), as well as the logic of the postulates themselves, are constituted from the relationships that the human being establishes with the earth.[37] Thus the basis of geometry is in human thought, and the human being's inquiries into geometrical relationships reveal more about the structure of the mind's sensibility than about the facts of an external world.[38] It follows that we will be more at home in the world the more we gain an understanding of the world.

But in apprehending the world by means of geometry we are simultaneously learning about ourselves. In this way, geometry is the common ground that connects the self to the world, providing an understandable context in which the self can dwell.[39]

Geometry exists independent of the contingent descriptions of the physical world that science offers. When we measure the earth we endow this with an order of our own devising. Within the context of our own order, the mutability of nature has a stable and predictable reference that helps remove it from the apparent workings of a capricious fate and situates it within the more predictable realm of human measure and order. It is easy to imagine that the cheer expressed by Aristippus in finding confirmation of the existence of an understandable order in the world was at least in part due to a realization that even the destructive act of nature represented by his shipwreck could be construed as merely an aberration in the ordered world of human purpose that he now found around him. There will be more shipwrecks, but these can now be attributed to human miscalculation rather than to an unkind or willful fate over which the human being has no understanding and therefore no control.

The Structure of the Cosmos

The human being brings to the world an impressive and effective system of spatial reasoning by which orientation for action is established. Its paradigms originate in the physical structure of the human figure and the less visible structure of the mind. But the world with which the human being contends possesses an equally authoritative structure all its own. This structure is different from that of the human being since its aims, although known only through conjecture, appear to be different from human aims.

For people to make a place, they search for correspondence between their own structure and that of the cosmos. For the human being, the structure of the cosmos begins with the opposition of day and night that is a consequence of the sun's course through the sky. While the sun's light makes biological life possible, it is the sun's circuit that makes possible the very idea of time and causes an indeterminate and formless expanse of space to become hierarchically divided to form meaningful places. It should be little surprise that creation legends characteristically begin with the dawn of light. While this literally allows people to see the new world into which they have come, more important is the consequent spatial and temporal structure that will be fundamental to the purposeful action that is the justification for the creation itself.[40]

If existence originates with the dawn of light, then the darkness that preceded this can only be associated literally and metaphorically with nonexistence or death. The possibility of a return to this state, as night falls and darkness returns, charges this occasion with anxiety. Thus it is the rhythm of the sun that provides the reference by which we reaffirm our own existence as we too wake from a dark unconsciousness to the beginning of a new day with the hopeful expectation that other days will follow. This daily reminder of the human struggle to overcome the limitations of individual mortality endows this twenty-four-hour cycle with moments of particular significance. With the rhythm of the sun, the activities that are necessary for our everyday existence can be ordered by the hierarchy already inherent in the day's structure. Through these predictable moments of congruence, the background patterns essential to sustain life are themselves registered as part of a larger purpose and elevated to something more special.

The rhythm of the sun establishes the daily cycle as the structure that most immediately orders human existence. But this daily structure is analogous to the seasonal cycle of birth, growth, death, and rebirth, so that the sun also becomes a daily reminder to the human being of the processes fundamental to nature. In constituting the world, the passage of time, which both science and history record as a fact of linear duration, is thus of less immediate value to the human being than the repeating patterns of daily, monthly, yearly, and generational cycles.[41] It should be obvious that building must take advantage of the sun's light and energy in order to most efficiently support the requisite needs of biological life. But architecture is expected to do more. Architecture makes a place for people by offering its own internal formal structure as both a reference to and a catalyst for the human being's speculation on the connections between the self and the cosmos. The consequent world that humans construe provides the stable structure by which we can plan our own existence. The rising and setting of the sun, despite its regular recurrence, can provide this stability only as the purposeful actions of people make its rhythms permanently present as a significant part of the structure that we constitute for ourselves.

The rising and setting of the sun not only orders human temporal existence, but simultaneously brings to presence a related system of spatial orientation.[42] The sun rises in the east, sets in the west, and has its noontime meridian (in the Northern Hemisphere) in the south. Thus, three of the four cardinal directions coincide with significant points in the sun's circuit. The earth now has its own spatial divisions, making an otherwise formless expanse into a differentiated system of places. These places are tangibly distinct due to the different quality of light that defines them as the sun moves through its daily path. Equally important, though, are the distinctions that derive from the fundamental opposition of day and night that so charges the human being's temporal structure with significance.

The east is the origin of the light that brings each new day into existence. This temporal origin establishes the east as a primary spatial reference by which the human being finds orientation in the world. Any activity that is situated relative to the east assumes a considerable degree of the hierarchical distinction that comes from the daily reminder of its housing the beginning of human existence. The common word for establishing one's bearings in the world, to *orient*, derives from the Latin *oriens* which means "rising" and refers to the eastern sunrise.[43] It is in the orient that Paradise was first located.[44]

The west is the place where the sun disappears. Its setting forebodes the return of darkness. While we have every expectation that the sun will rise again, the coming of night always carries with it a certain anxiety. The Latin verb *occido,* from which derives *occident* for the western direction, means "to set" but also "to die." The sun's circuit therefore establishes the poles of human existence each day. But these poles are not isolated or disconnected from one another. The sun, determining this duality, is also the link between them.

North, the fourth cardinal point, although not directly determined by the sun, is implicated as part of the north to south axis around which the earth rotates (and around which the universe also was once thought to rotate). This axis becomes significant as the stable armature that holds together the structure of the earth and relates all places to this center. The north, however, is made known to the human being at night when Polaris, the stationary north star, points to the north pole of this armature.

The Romans made all of this quite clear when they laid out the foundations for their towns.[45] Here, center was determined as a consequence of two axes crossing at right angles. The *cardo*, which was the main north to south street, means "axle" and refers to the axis around which the universe rotates. The main east to west street, the *decumanus*, is related to the path of the sun as it rises and sets. The Roman town, therefore, was given a secure place in the world as it replicated the structure of the cosmos, and its buildings could be situated and constructed so as to participate in and further qualify the meanings of this structure.[46]

The cosmos is construed by humans from the world that receives us. We compare and contrast what we know of ourselves with what we observe of the world, and make hypotheses about probable relationships. In this way a world without form, a world of circumstances, is reconstituted as a world with structure and order and ultimately a world with purpose. This is the cosmos or the construed world that is the basis for human settlement.

Human settlement becomes significant as it is demarcated explicitly or implicitly according to the structure of these paradigms, and human existence becomes meaningful as an outcome of the intentional orientation of human action within this hierarchy. While it might be argued that these paradigms are now so conventionalized that they must fail to correspond to the conditions of the present, the process of human intellection persists in measuring and evaluating the world by means of structures that have remained constant for as long as the human being has left artifacts that represent the inhabited world. The center of the human being's world might no longer coincide with the axis of the universe, it might no longer be capable of being the sole point of reference for a complex existence; but a world with no idea of center could only signal an entropic lack of differentiation that means a world exhausted. These paradigms have endured as the reference by which the world is construed; it is up to us to continue to use them well.

"And since they were of an imitative and teachable nature, they would daily point out to each other the results of their building, boasting of the novelties in it; and thus, with their natural gifts sharpened by emulation, their standards improved daily." *Drawing by Celia Liu.*

5

Constructing the Paradigm

Vitruvius's account of the materials and techniques used to construct the first dwelling is indeed curious. In what could have been a simple description of the human being's first attempts to build a primitive shelter, we find ambitious intentions extending well beyond the usual considerations of crafting an artifact. By taking the process of constructing out of the private realm, where it would be of little theoretical or philosophical interest, and presenting it as a public activity, Vitruvius gives to this simple and instrumental activity a purpose commensurate with its new location within the place of gathering. Constructing can now be considered as part of public life and can be discussed in ways parallel to that other public activity he describes: the building of a language. This change in venue reframes the question of constructing and situates its intentions within the broader discourse defining the purpose of human settlement.

In his introduction to the study of architecture, Vitruvius compiles an impressive and comprehensive list of disciplines the knowledge of which is essential to the making of architecture. It would seem unlikely that so many disciplines could ever be mastered by the architect. Yet Vitruvius observes that "all studies have a common bond of union and intercourse with one another" and that one who receives instruction in these various fields will "recognize the same stamp on all the arts . . . and so . . . more readily comprehend them all."[1] The various disciplines of learning were all part of a single body of knowledge and all shared the common purpose of interpreting the world to make it habitable. It is important to remember that this observation was made within an intellectual context different from ours. Vitruvius was writing when the sciences were far more closely allied with what we now think of as the liberal arts. Physics, for example, was a branch of knowledge within the discipline of philosophy. Hence it is not necessarily surprising when he explains that human progress is directly attributable to the particular mental acuity that is catalyzed by and advanced through the activities of constructing. Vitruvius's human being, already distinguished from the other animals by "its mind having been equipped with the power of thought and understanding . . . gradually advanced from the construction of buildings to the other arts and sciences, and so passed from a rude and barbarous mode of life to civilization and refinement."[2] In other words, construction is the medium through which the human being is enabled to define civilization.

This high regard that Vitruvius displays toward constructing—at odds with its current status as an instrumental activity—suggests that we reexamine the possibilities inherent in the idea. The word *construct* reveals the potential for more ambitious intentions through a fundamental ambiguity. Derived from the Latin *construere,* construct means "to heap together, to pile up, or to fit together."[3] The emphasis is on the parts, whose assembly is directed more from a logic inherent in the part itself than from a purpose defined in the consequent assembled artifact. Stated differently, this meaning suggests that we can know how to pile up or fit together these parts but are without knowledge of exactly what we are making. This meaning does not support Vitruvius's confidence that constructing will help to constitute a sophisticated civilization. In his definition, construction must be capable of directing purposeful action beyond the piling up of parts.

The ambiguity in the term *construct* comes from a second meaning which, in combination with the first, substantiates Vitruvius's confidence. To construe, one of the roots of construct, means "to interpret, to put a meaning on or to explain."[4] This more synthetic description suggests the primacy of the completed work in construction, since the whole must exist axiologically prior to the parts to be rendered susceptible to interpretation. This qualification shifts attention away from the parts and gives to the whole the task of directing its own assembly. This whole, being both the sum of its many constituent parts and an entity in its own right, is capable of transcending these pieces. It is able to be fully understood or explained only as it is taken apart in an examination of the means through which the revealed pieces (themselves endowed with purpose under the first definition) contribute to this whole. The part can now be compared with the whole to understand specific instances of reinforced or qualified intentions, which makes the whole entity more articulate and rich in meaning. The fundamental ambiguity in the way construction can be understood (based in the logic of its parts or on the completed entity toward which work is directed) thus endows both part and whole with purpose, and allows for a certain independence of each from the other even as they both contribute to a shared end. It is with this understanding of constructing that Vitruvius describes the interaction between the ideas and values of the arts and sciences, which put together a view of the world, and the ideas and values of architecture, where constructions give another point of access to the structure of the cosmos.[5]

Constructing must be both a synthetic and an analytic activity.[6] In a synthetic mode, the human being is putting together a complete world in order to secure a place within it. This world becomes believable as a guide for action to the degree that it appears a unity, holding together both intellectually and physically. This is the role of paradigmatic structure, which is always directed toward unity, synthesis, and closure. The world that it reveals is a cosmos whose synthetic unity can subsume ourselves and an unmediated nature within its own order.

Human existence, however, is sufficiently complex and surprising to be resistent to the reductive simplification necessary to achieve this paradigmatic coherence. Furthermore, the necessary completeness of the paradigm itself precludes any easy analytic disassembly, keeping it uncomfortably distant and seemingly inscrutable to an inquiring gaze. Finally, humans cannot generally be expected to take on the world as a totality. Instead, we engage pieces of it, optimistically anticipating and therefore projecting a more comprehensive structure from these pieces. Therefore, in addition to a synthetic vision we also need to be able to approach the world through an analytical process. We need some way to imagine how the world might be put together from pieces whose existence, if they could be revealed, would disclose the many decisions and judgments that support the whole. This is not a simple analytic process, because the constituent parts of construction tend to be masked by the conflicting need for the whole constructed work to be rendered with a degree of closure appropriate for it to represent a stable world. Yet if the pieces of a constructed artifact were also revealed as entities in their own right, this independence would momentarily free them from the whole, to be reconstituted synthetically in a new construct. This construct could now include both the human being and the circumstances under which this new synthesis had been engaged. At this moment of mentally grasping the making of things through recognizing the individual parts, the human being would enter into a substantial relationship with the world.[7]

Reviewing this expanded definition of constructing and its role in our ability to understand the world, we find that the decisions or judgments from which the world is constituted must be accessible, recoverable, and subject to critical understanding. This requires a structure whose unity will remain intact and evident, but one that is also articulate so that it can reveal at the same time the individual voices of the parts. (It is worth noting that "articulate" has both linguistic and constructional implications, since it refers to "speaking clearly" as well as to "uniting by means of a joint.")[8]

Constructing must therefore respond to the apparent paradox between the need to make present the physical manifestations of a stable and coherent world and the need to reveal the discontinuities and junctures in the underlying paradigms that make this world accessible to the human being. The terms "discontinuity" and "juncture" require some explanation in order to elucidate the nature of this paradox.

"Discontinuity" describes a condition that will most typically occur within a part of the paradigm, whereas "juncture" describes a condition in the relationship between the parts. An example of the former is the break in continuity in a boundary such as a wall through which the passage of a door or window is made. At a window or door the primary objective of this boundary—the securing of a distinction between the inside and the outside—is rendered vulnerable by the necessity for actual physical connection between these disparate worlds. It is at this intersection between passage and boundary, two conditions that describe contradictory relationships between the inside and outside, that one constructs the entry. The boundary, which at the moment of entry is mostly vestigial, must be made present to remind us of its prior ability to literally separate these realms. The passage, which actually allows one to move between worlds previously kept apart, must demonstrate the continuing importance of the violated boundary by making the passage difficult. The entry requires its multiple and redundant articulation in response to its ambiguous situation. By simultaneously regulating the degree of separation or connection within both the boundary and the passage, and revealing and articulating the expected distinctions between the two, one can achieve great spatial clarity at this point of disjunction. Thus one becomes able to represent a particular institution's location within the public hierarchy of institutions and the relationship that this institution wishes to achieve relative to the world of nature. One is also able to provide the appropriate degree of physical or metaphysical security. The fact that these tasks are not always coextensive often renders the construction of the entry quite interesting.

For an example of the juncture between parts of the paradigm we can consider the relationship between the wall and the ground plane, or between the wall and the sky surrogates of roof and ceiling. In each case, two sets of boundaries constituting different conditions of being inside and outside can be joined, kept apart, or engaged in a dialogue. The wall's base meets the boundary of the ground plane or terrace that will distinguish existence on the earth from that of the underground. The wall's top meets the ceiling, roof, or cornice, all of which establish the boundary that comes between the human being and the sky. The constructional articulation at the wall's base must support the wall and ground it in its particular place. It can also reveal the degree to which the imagined underground might safely be permitted to be present in the everyday life carried out on the earth's surface. Likewise, the difficulty of the passage between earth and firmament (a passage more frequently metaphorical than actual) is represented by the constructional articulation of cornices, reveals, and crown moldings, all of which suggest the continuing upward extension of the wall and yet also provide the cap that keeps this extension grounded.[9]

These moments of discontinuity and juncture are critical, because they provide the location in which the actions of the human being are related to the constructional facts of building. At these moments, the unselfconscious guide of the paradigm is raised to consciousness, and we are able to inspect it and to speculate about its meaning. We engage particular manifestations of its structure that otherwise are hidden within the unity of the whole through these constructed discontinuities and junctures. Human action and the facts of building converge, allowing the synthetic structure of the paradigm to become the means by which the order of our world is revealed.

Consider, for instance, the moment when a person grasps the handle to open a door. At this instant the human's measure is placed upon the building. The height of the handle, its position relative to the door's axis of pivot, the form of the handle itself, and the mechanics of its action are the immediate, palpable means by which we measure ourselves against the building. The framing of the door surround that supports the pierced wall and seals its exposed edges from dirt and rain must, at the same time, represent the wall's fundamental role in maintaining the construed distinction between inside and outside. Here, the head of the door or lintel and the jambs (legs) on which it rests form a structure with explicit analogies to the particular strengths of the human body that might resist the wall's implicit collapse. This analogy further engages the human as both the instigator of the wall's breach and the metaphorical means by which this breach can be mended. The doorway reveals other allegiances as it is seen as an aedicule, or little building, which itself possesses the integrity and coherence of the much larger world to be entered.[10] These critical moments become microcosms representing the larger whole. In the example of the entry, the idea of passage might be elongated into an extended processional movement, but it could alternatively be condensed into the articulation of the door jamb. In this way constructing is able to represent the larger purpose of the whole, establishing a secure location for the human being within its hierarchy.

Paradoxically, it is through the apparent frailty of discontinuity and juncture that we achieve a more firm grasp on the idea of a stable and coherent world. This paradox disappears only after we have acknowledged that there is significant value in our persistent inability to resolve the disaccord between the human desire for collective stability and the volatility of individual will. With this acknowledgment comes our awareness that it is the task of constructing to represent this precarious relationship, rather than to attempt an implausible and premature resolution. The particular locus for this constructional task is the institution.[11]

The idea of the institution can be elucidated by referring once more to the Vitruvian gathering in the forest. As the assembled group became too large to allow all of the individuals to know each other, smaller ("building and boasting") groups would inevitably form. The institution is a means through which these groups bring order to their gatherings. In much the same way that Vitruvius describes the process of inaugurating the first dwelling, we could imagine individuals, already aware of the advantages of the polity, replicating appropriate aspects of its purpose and structure in order to serve a shared goal that contributes to the larger polity. This appropriated mental structure, assuming physical form through the process of construction, gives a place to each individual within the emerging institution and provides the stability needed for these individuals to make decisions and judgments about their role within the polity. In this way, the institution is the exemplary means through which constructing becomes a public activity, thus potentially allowing for Vitruvius's ambitious description of architecture to be fulfilled.

The synthetic structure of the paradigm establishes the fundamental relationships among people, their institutions, and nature. The most important public institutions, for example, are likely to be located at a public center. This center would be situated to reveal the salient geographical or ecological characteristics—height, prospect, orientation, or associational implication—that would have attracted settlement in the first place.[12] These institutions would then be housed within places whose figural identity is ordered by the inherent hierarchy of geometrical structures or by means of conventional association, thereby distinguishing themselves among each other and isolating them from the supporting background of the private realm. Constructing reveals these institutional hierarchies through its ability to realize the appropriate paradigmatic structures to house and represent these institutions.[13]

Yet for the assembled individuals to persist as an enduring and stable polity, these institutional traces of their collective values and accomplishments must survive beyond the span of a human generation. The permanence of these reminders of a collective past demonstrates a commitment to the future and provides encoded values to act as its guide.[14] But this permanence can never be absolute nor pervasive. People need to decide the degree to which each of their political institutions must remain resistant to contingency and, therefore, the relative significance accorded to each. This, of course, can be seen as the purpose of gathering.

Architecture, or for that matter any artifact, is elevated to the degree that it appears to permanently resist both physical and political contingency. This resistance is obviously necessary at a literal level (the building must remain structurally sound and not be rendered obsolete by inevitable changes in use) but is equally important at the level of representation. A building should last as long as the purpose that initiated its foundation, and it must unequivocally communicate this commitment publicly. The materials of building already possess intrinsic characteristics such as durability, resilience, and resistance to various stresses that suggest the limits under which they might be used. These intrinsic properties are combined with qualities associated with the human intervention needed to free the material from the earth and to render it suitable for building. In the preindustrial world, the degree of difficulty with which a material was extracted from its natural situation was nearly proportional to its eventual stature as a building material. Therefore, stone generally ranked higher than brick, brick higher than mud, and large stones tended to command greater respect than smaller ones.[15] An extension of this hierarchy is the value that accrues to workmanship. The care and effort required to produce a fine surface, while often contributing to a material's actual strength, is more an index to the strength of the belief that endurance itself is important, revealing that this particular example and the institution of which it is a part are indeed intended to endure.[16]

But is it possible or even useful to think of endurance in absolute terms? Very few programs will command the degree of permanence found, for instance, at the great pyramids, which were required to protect and preserve the body of a quasi god forever, providing its soul a place to return and thus assuring the soul's immortality. Very few individuals or even governments will ever again be able to command the resources to attempt such a feat. Permanence is best measured on a less absolute scale. In fact the absolute singularity of purpose that drove the conception of the pyramid is rarely encountered in political institutions as they have been known in the intervening millennia. Institutions, by their very nature, are not rigidly monolithic nor are they inflexibly autonomous. These qualities, while initially important for an institution's identity and authority, can only be achieved by a reductive simplification that if left unchecked would undermine both.

This curious relationship between authority and reductive clarity in an institution parallels that of the paradigm, the mental structure through which the physical structure of the institution is realized. The coherence in the structure of the paradigm, and the distinction between this structure and the requisite chaos that surrounds it, are indeed achieved by reducing the complexity of the patterns of human relatedness to structures more readily able to remind and guide people's actions in a world whose order is not so immediately apparent. Under the auspices of pure paradigmatic clarity, the simple is appreciated more than the complicated, independence and autonomy more than connectedness, and linear relationships more than networks or webs. Yet if this reductive state were all, the effective longevity of the paradigm would be severely tested. The paradigm offers authority, not the power required to maintain a reductive order in place. The paradigm can remain vital only as it is able to respond to the repeated challenges brought to it by the world out there, a world of circumstance. The capacity of this paradigm to be transformed and enlarged, and even to subsume ideas seemingly contrary to its initial structure without collapse, is the reason for its persistence. The authority held out by any paradigm is ultimately due to the effectiveness with which it allows succeeding generations to see themselves in the world and to act in accordance with this vision. This must never be mistaken for the exercise of power, whether sinister or benign.

The limitations of the paradigm must be acknowledged, so that its authority allows for the individual exercise of free will. The abstract, generalized, and public nature of the paradigm, all conditions essential to its ability to provide a stable world in which the individual's identity is safe, are also conditions that tend to limit this individual exercise of free will. While unrestrained individual freedom fails to provide a context sufficient for political stability, its suppression can be viewed only with equal alarm. Yet we are not left with a choice between irreconcilable extremes. Fundamental to human existence, from the moment we left the forest and made a place in the world, has been the burden, willingly assumed, of distinguishing our existence from another way of being in the world that we viewed as lacking in significant purpose. The problem, however, was that this other way was our own nature as an individual animal in the forest. The dilemma that this recognition presents has been the basis for much philosophical thought and architectural action. Yet rather than accepting a choice between the freedom of the individual and a singular authority, it would be more appropriate to acknowledge the validity of both conditions. It is through the subtle nuances of potential connections between paradigms, rather than in reductive simplifications, that the anxious condition of being human might be celebrated.[17]

An examination of the overlap between paradigms is thus useful and interesting. If the articulation of this layering—in construction revealed as points of discontinuity and juncture—becomes as valid an architectural project as the maintenance of a monolithic paradigmatic coherence, then the stature of the parts is elevated until these are revealed as entities in their own right. As such they are able to engage in their own relationships with the individual, the landscape, and other institutions. At this level of articulation, the institution transcends the limits of its public role and can become a significant part of each human's existence.[18]

Once the institution is securely situated in its political setting through a reductive process, it should be possible to reconsider the relationships that establish its position and identity. These relationships, initially set up to distinguish clearly between the institution and its political and physical context, achieve this distinction by establishing an artificial polarity that often masks or suppresses equally important connections and dependencies. For example, the initial distinction between the public and private realms is needed to establish a context with greater authority than the separate initiatives of isolated individuals. The distinction establishes the validity of the public world of debate and consensus, and simultaneously legitimizes the sanctity of private thoughts and actions. The private world must be protected so that the independent initiatives nurtured there can arrive in the public world in full force.[19] Thus, the relationship between public and private worlds proves to be one of some mutual dependence, and not simply a hierarchical privileging of the public. It is a curious and not

immediately expected outcome that the greater the hierarchical distinction of public over private, the greater will be the recognition of
the achievement of the individual in moving successfully between these
two realms.

Vitruvius has described how individuals, while constructing the first
houses within the recently achieved security of the clearing, pointed
to and publicly boasted of the virtues of each innovation. Those private
innovations that withstood public scrutiny were incorporated within
the body of norms whose standards Vitruvius describes as rising daily.
Vitruvius does not indicate closure on these standards but describes a
public process by which a tradition of building is constantly made new.

Likewise, the autonomy that insulates an institution from contingency, and helps to establish an unequivocal hierarchical identity
within the public realm, cannot be absolute.[20] In order to define the
full breadth of human existence, the less predictably stable web of
human interconnectedness must find a way to assert itself. This must
occur despite the immanent completion of the paradigm, which tends
to disengage the institution from its political and physical context. The
boundary that secures and represents the independence of the institution therefore must become articulate. The differentiated parts that
are revealed within the boundary's structure through articulation now
become able to suggest recombination with parts of the previously excluded context. Additional purposes can now be proposed for the institution as it becomes increasingly engaged in the larger world. The
initial representation of autonomy and independence provides a public armature around which the more fleeting and perhaps private relationships are gathered, given protection, and, without compromising
the institution, are shown to be important in their own right. It is in
this way that the security of a bounded world promotes the human's
probing of the limits of this world. The institution must of course have
an inherent structural mechanism allowing it to grow in response to
this probing, otherwise its authority will not persist.

The representation of an absolute and monolithic permanence is
contrary to the inevitable changes that accompany the human's constant inquiry into the world. Many of the conclusions of these inquiries
will remain short-lived and must have the means to be valued as such.
Occasionally, however, their import is such that the original paradigm

must respond in some substantial way or itself lose authority. This, problematically, would suggest that the permanent is necessarily dependent on the ephemeral. The idea of permanence must be thought of as articulate and capable of differentiation in order to accommodate and represent a stable and enduring institutional corpus that is constituted from very ephemeral arrangements.[21] Again we confront the paradox of the paradigm, where the most tangible manifestations of its existence are found in the accommodation of the most ephemeral uses, themselves a response to the constantly changing contingencies of a particular time and place. How can this constant flux ever represent the degree of permanence so necessary to the stability of the institution? The representation of permanence is possible only when one distinguishes between the purpose of the institution and the functions necessary to sustain this purpose. Purpose will almost certainly have its basis in a political ideal and be understood through enduring structures that establish the relationships among people and between people and the landscapes within which they dwell. It is these more enduring structures that sponsor and in turn are supported by the myriad functions necessary to sustain everyday life. These functions are important both on their own and in relation to the institution. They must be accommodated in such a way that their more transient life is recognized and given its appropriate value, but without compromising the representation of the more stable purpose of the institution.

In making this distinction between purpose and function, it is possible to look again to the paradigm for help. The degree to which an institution is able to order its own existence so that it resists the contingencies of changing use and other external pressures determines its situation within the public hierarchy of institutions. The greatest resistance is possible when the institution is represented by paradigmatic structures independent of these changing uses and whose own order is recognized as an a priori ideal. For example, the center is an ideal that in some way must always be acknowledged. The center might promote gathering or deliberative assembly or it might accommodate private contemplation. It might even forego the direct accommodation of political action and represent the possibility of this totemically. As the purpose of the institution becomes more overlaid with purposes defined within the other institutions that make up the web of human relations, its structure will likewise become more complex. The center must now represent an oscillating allegiance among various institutions and might assume a more deliberatively ambiguous or diffuse presence, possibly dividing into more than one center. The idea of the center, much like the purpose of the institution, is initially simple. And yet it is this fundamental clarity of order and intent that gives to each the ability to become elaborate and articulate in response to the contrary demands of human existence.[22]

Constructing must establish the conditions for this stability. It must do this by transcending its own factual and material limitations in order to represent a more enduring permanence.[23] Since all institutions, by their nature, are founded on the belief that they will endure forever and consequently expect to be represented as such, they require the stability intrinsic to paradigmatic structures like the center to carry this representational burden. These paradigms are effective due to their abstract and universal nature, which also is one of the reasons that significant institutions within diverse cultures at different historical moments are so structurally similar. For instance, the frequency with which the circle is found fulfilling this representational role is a direct result of its own abstract geometrical structure and its already enumerated virtues of nearly absolute resistance to contingent deformation. If these abstract ideas of geometric resistance found within the circle, or to a lesser degree in other geometrical figures, are to remain persuasive in their representation of institutional endurance, then it is critical that their embodiment be made manifest in a system of constructing that would offer little or no access to the literal or material mechanisms of its own assembly. Thus the means of making this paradigm present become as inscrutably dense as possible so as to offer almost no opening to subsequent challenge. In this way the idea of endurance is able to transcend as much as possible the intellectual and material limitations that otherwise would almost certainly raise doubts. This singularly purposeful circle gains its stability through an equally purposeful abstraction, as it draws far away from the representation of anything specific that would render it vulnerable.

This intense abstraction, however, should not be thought of as the goal of architecture. Having achieved the security of reductive stability, one should have the confidence to reconsider what might have been suppressed in the process of abstraction, and to allow this as well to be revealed. It is at this moment that an authentically ambiguous condition is created, in which both a reductive and an elaborative description of the institution coexist. In the reductive version, the institution is clearly hierarchical, exclusive of most contingency, and operating within a system of public values. The elaborative version will be characterized more as a web or network of tentative private relations, with no one piece attracting particular attention to itself. Their coexistence suggests the problematic condition faced by architecture in constructing the world. On one hand it must represent the universal qualities that any institution must to some degree possess in order to be instantly registered by a potentially uninterested public. On the other hand, it must respond to the myriad particularities that make this institution special for each participating individual.

If we return to the circle, however, we find a paradigmatic structure that can only represent a reductive account of this world. The solution to this apparent limitation is the use of multiple and redundant structures to reinforce the original reductive paradigm, as well as to confront this with alternative allegiances that extend the institution to the wider audience excluded by the initial process of abstraction. Since most geometrical figures share certain fundamental properties with each other, it is possible to layer these figures on one another. At the critical points where the figures intersect, the new hybrid figure can allow moments of congruence as well as divergence to be reinforced or suppressed.

The architect's responsibility is to establish the relationship between these opposed conditions so that the resulting structure is able to accommodate the conflicting values that each represents. A simple example would be the center represented by a circle inscribed within a square. To a large extent both figures define a similar relationship between an implied center and its explicit boundary. Yet the square, by applying an elementary transformation or translating one of its sides to a position beyond the original edge, can be opened to actual or implied attachment to other figures.[24] It is open to part of the field previously excluded from its domain. It may even be open to a world beyond the stated boundaries of the institution. While this challenges the square's original closure, the seemingly redundant structure of the circle, with its stronger sense of unity, remains stable even while it is substantially engaged in the square's own constitutional geometry. This simple example describes a condition of stability coexisting with one of extension and vulnerability and shows that architecture's paradigms can indeed be inclusive of a wide range of meaning.

Further extension of this example could suggest that square and circle potentially operate on quite different temporal scales. The square, in accommodating contextual and individual initiatives, increasingly relinquishes its hold on these more ephemeral arrangements as they achieve a more permanent connection to the center. If the inevitable changes that these arrangements undergo can be accommodated and brought into relationship with the stabilizing capacity of the abstract idea of center without seriously compromising the institution itself, then it is likely that this institution will endure.

The institution also becomes the place where a polity approaches conclusions about distinction between the world of the human and that of nature. Vitruvius describes how the polity of human settlement is possible only after the solitary human has left the forest for a world constituted through the authority of public gathering. This coincides with the significant shift away from an instinctual behavior driven by the necessity of individual physical survival to intentional human action. The political, social, and cultural world of the human begins at this moment. The tenuous nature of the achievement of intentional action, however, is already evident in the device of the fire. Although initially a frightening product of the natural processes of the forest, the fire eventually becomes the catalyst for and the protector of the public assembly. This equivocal situation only becomes problematic, however, if the artifice of the human world is taken to be irrevocably polarized with respect to the world of nature. The distinctions that Vitruvius makes are not antinomic. The fire is allowed to oscillate between the natural and human worlds, as it reveals to each what the other is not. The boundary between the human and natural worlds is also uncertain. Physically it exists as the edge of the forest that remains after the fire's destruction has created its fortuitous clearing. But does a reliance on a boundary not of human making diminish the authority of this boundary, bringing into question the human being's capacity to secure its world though its own devices? If so, then we must look to the center, expecting here a less enigmatic means by which the human being could demarcate so critical a boundary. Again we find the problematic fire, whose light and radiating warmth caused people to gather around it and implicitly define the limits of the clearing as the consequent circle of humans, themselves positioned relative to some invisible circumference beyond which the benefits of the fire are lost. Although this edge can now be thought to be unequivocally of human origin, one's satisfaction can only be momentary. Satisfaction gives way to doubt as soon as attention returns to the natural presence of the fire at the center of the clearing.

Finding it difficult to maintain a distinction between the construed world of human action and the world of nature should not, however, be cause for alarm. The two worlds are inextricably engaged, forming a complex structure within which human existence unfolds. The distinction that the human being so carefully erects must always be recognized as provisional. This artifice is essential for the human being's security. It establishes a boundary to the domain over which we can expect to have a sufficiently reliable knowledge to guide our existence. But by establishing limits, humans are also setting out the conditions under which we will eventually transgress these limits and test our own knowledge against a world that we recognize as holding answers to many of the questions that at any particular time elude us.

The distinction we make between the natural and human worlds is strong and durable, as witnessed by the ingenuity and variety of its forms. This powerful distinction is precisely commensurate with the recognition a human being is awarded for transcending so powerful a divide, and with the great value we accord to the discovery that in yet another way the human being is able to coexist with the world of nature. As the Vitruvian example shows, whenever we try to define a limit between the human being's world and the world of nature, we may discover instead an interpretive oscillation between them. The task of constructing is to represent such oscillations within an articulate structure that both accommodates and represents our inquiries into our problematic situation within the world of nature. In the same way that the institution itself cannot be considered to be monolithic, its architecture must remain articulate. The columns, walls, beams, floors, ceilings, and roofs need not conform to a subsuming Cartesian and material homogeneity, but could reveal an institution responding to the complexities of its many constituencies.

At this point one can make inferences about the nature of the ambitious task Vitruvius assigns to constructing. The scope of this task is founded in the complexity of the human world. This complexity begins with the fundamental tension intrinsic to our uneasy situation on the earth as one of the beasts, yet unique by virtue of our unwillingness to accept our placement here as fate. The world the human being construes is problematic, since we must acknowledge our own tenuous and provisional accommodation within the other world of nature while simultaneously proposing hypotheses to overcome this. The consequent construct holds together only to the extent that the idea of its imputed structure is substantially greater than the sum of its recognizable parts. This is the guarantee that our continuing project to render our order manifest will not disintegrate leaving us without purpose.

Attempts to reduce the world to simple terms therefore will rarely meet with any long-lasting satisfaction. While we are aware of this dilemma, we still know no other way to proceed. This is not necessarily a problem, as long as we recognize that the paradigms we rely on to grasp the immensity of the world are representations and not substitutes for the world.

The paradigm's capacity for representation and its durability reside to a considerable degree in its evanescence. Although possessing an unequivocal authority, assured by the coherence of its internal structure, it is without any concrete corporal existence of its own. Rather, it is known by inference as an armature, implicated by what it seems capable of holding together. Its structure begins to be revealed through evidence deduced from the accumulating actions gathered about it. Each time something new is identified as a possible part of its constellation, the idea of the paradigm is enlarged and further explicated by the specificity of the transformations the human being proposes as necessary to accommodate what is known of the new piece. Therefore, it is the collaboration between the stabilizing yet evanescent paradigm and the boundless elaborative potential of the human that ensures its continuing vitality. To take advantage of this elaborative energy, the paradigm must be intensely engaged in the public discourse that is at the foundation of any human settlement and out of which are constituted public and private institutions.

The polity that Vitruvius describes is possible only because the making of its own architecture prompts questions that must be resolved through public debate. Although the fire established the context for the first gathering and provided its focus, this unselfconscious coming together was without recognizable structure until the humans' disinterested wordplay advanced to the public naming of things and thus initiated speech. Public assembly is constituted at this intersection of action and speech, and its consequent structure is recognized as a product of human intention. Constructing and speaking are intimately entangled in making the human world. It is through constructing that these primitive people are shown advancing to a refined civilization, and it is through speech, as they point and boast about each new innovation, that their primitive shelters become part of a sophisticated public architecture.

Under the protection and guidance of the paradigm, public discourse is possible. The paradigm's intrinsic stability provides the context for an ordered public discourse, and its acknowledged limits instigate the specific means by which the individual transcends and therefore enlarges this discourse. Constructing reveals the paradigm's structure as articulate and allows the exposed pieces to further engage in relationships beyond those it initially prescribes. Thus this discourse becomes rich: capable of representing the almost limitless intentions of the assembled individuals as they build the world.

Constructed articulation must be capable of revealing many layers of order. Human settlement and its institutions are constructed, paradoxically, as they are taken apart to reveal the constellation of possible relationships within. Since human existence is both complex and ambiguous, the constructed discontinuities and junctures that uncouple these layered paradigms must be able to reveal the nuances, subtleties in gradation, and contradictions that give this existence its continuing richness. Moreover, the development of a civilization must be accompanied by an increasingly fine scale of differentiation made within relationships that once were considered to be synonymous. Lastly, as one shifts from the public to private within a particular institution, the possible relationships in which people might engage are further increased as the more fluid web of private connection displaces the linear hierarchy of the public realm.

Architecture must have the capacity to make these possibilities present to a public that will encounter its works under rather diverse circumstances over a long period of time. But architecture, as we have already seen, cannot accomplish this if it becomes a substitute that reduces the human's world to a collection of signs. The resulting specificity limits the extent to which we can bring our own meanings and find a resonance between these and a receptive architecture. Yet without our continuing engagement, architecture will indeed revert to an assemblage of signs that will be emptied of meaning well before the artifact deteriorates, leaving it remote from human experience.

Within the security of the paradigm, the human world is thus best understood as a world in need of elaboration. Rather than fixing on a singular and isolated description by which the world makes some limited, instrumental sense, we make hypotheses about its structure from the myriad relationships we enter into with it. By comparing our accumulating experiences and thoughts with one another relative to a preexistent structure or paradigm, we become able to maintain a grasp on the rapidly expanding world.

The human being's capacity to abstract allows each particular experience or thought to reveal a typical quality. Abstraction enables the human being to establish the similarities and isolate the differences that support the effective comparison among a diverse array of experiences. As raw experience is abstracted into typical structures, there is a further drawing away from the initial, extrinsic referent so that the intrinsic relationships of these structures are able to engage each other more freely without the full encumbrance of conventional attributions of content. In this way, the human being participates in a complex and open set of relationships whose recombinant possibilities reveal the potential structure of a parallel world. Thus architecture becomes a coherent world of its own, providing the structure through which the unselfconscious behavior of daily existence can be given measure and order, transcending the contingencies of survival to become the purposeful action out of which the world is construed.

Simultaneous with this process of drawing away from the concrete to form the paradigm is the process of constructing. Our constructions represent the structure of the paradigm and reveal its discontinuities. Also, due to the necessity that construction must house specific activities and be formed from specific materials, these artifices supply the clues that link the abstract structure of the paradigm back to a recognizable world of human experience. These clues still are not uniquely coupled to a singular referent, but exhibit a considerable degree of overlap and redundancy. Thus they are able to announce their specific intentions without necessarily limiting the domain over which these intentions might prevail.

The wall provides an example of the expressive possibilities of such constructed clues. The actual materials out of which a wall might be constructed will be selected to hold up and shelter the institution during its intended life. But the wall has many additional roles to fulfill as it participates in the separation and eventual connection of the inside and outside worlds which are constituted as distinct by the actions of the paradigm's boundary. Therefore, without rendering the material false, it is necessary to transcend its actuality in order for the consequent artifice to acquire a more articulate voice.[25] This is evident in the convention of the fictive joint pattern, rendered so that the scale of the wall is elevated beyond the size of the actual constructional unit. For this to be effective requires that some distance be gained from material fact in order that the consequent abstraction can represent the more difficult metaphorical protection that the boundary of the paradigm demands. But the acknowledged artifice of these massive blocks of stone, when further possessed of a surface only a scant remove from raw nature, signals the convention of rustication which, additionally, establishes a new relation between the building and the earth. The wall's surface, however, is not the only place where the paradigm's qualifications are present. These are also represented at the entry, where the wall's thickness is revealed through passage. They are represented in the elaboration of the juncture between the wall and the earth, which also establishes the relationship between the underground and life on earth. Finally, these qualifications can be represented at the corners, where constructional emphasis such as the use of quoins actually and figuratively strengthens the effect of the wall while indicating a degree of detachment necessary for an institution located in this physical setting. It is the redundancy of these clues and their ability to shift allegiance among the many parts of the paradigm that gives architecture its capacity to be continually open to the inquiries made by a changing public audience. This capacity to remain open should not be mistaken for the lack of will to take a stand. It is in fact the willing embrace of the difficult that allows the paradigm to truly accommodate and represent the goals and aspirations of people when faced with the contrariness and difficulty of a rich and varied existence.

Architecture is a discipline complementary to the language that the assembled people learned to speak. The articulation of construction, combined with the practical purpose that these constructions serve, becomes the means by which we represent our understanding of ourselves in the world. We are nearly two thousand years removed from the time when Vitruvius envisioned the possibility of architecture engaging the issues facing humanity through articulate construction. Yet we find ourselves similarly in need of the vital architecture through which he hoped to establish and represent a public realm for the Roman citizen. We live in a world where discourse has been reduced to the monolithic polar opposites of the political slogan, increasingly dogmatic and incapable of resolution. Our world is desperately in need of elaboration. It is a world in need of a public realm with an engaged public, where issues can be discussed and resolved by actual and metaphorical constructions.

Epilogue

Writing at the end of the second millennium, we perhaps are no wiser than either Vitruvius or his fictive dwellers. We have, however, inherited the world that is the inevitable consequence of their thoughts and actions. We should be prompted to look at this world to ask whether it is the world we would have willed. It is difficult to imagine that we could ever answer in the affirmative. The immediacy of the present always prevents the distance necessary to understand its direction. The resultant melange of disconnected fragments is rarely viewed with optimism. The persistence of this predicament of the present makes the intellectual achievements of humanity more remarkable. Maxim Gorky's observation that life will always be bad enough never to extinguish humanity's desire for something better is borne out by the history of philosophical, artistic, and scientific endeavor. Our present is no different. The evidence seems to point to a world that will soon be incapable of sustaining itself. Even the most superficial analysis produces a list of social, political, environmental, and health afflictions, a list profoundly depressing not only for its size but also for its dizzying diversity. How could we imagine a beginning that might address in some significant manner even one of these ills, much less the whole panoply? That we are always willing to assume this responsibility is a consequence of our being endowed with the unique gift of thinking ourselves capable of beginning again. Beginning again grants us freedom from the tyranny of time, the seemingly purposeless but relentless unfolding of history, and the supposed irreversibility of science. Through this freedom we are able to make hypotheses about the symptoms of a problematic present that place the present within the more optimistic paradigms that we devise to make the world. This is exactly what is offered by revisiting Vitruvius's tale of origins.

We begin again, however, with several crucial assumptions about the constancy of these paradigms that allow us to recognize in both the Vitruvian context and our immediate present the shared conditions that reveal meaningful difference. The centered structure of human perception and the repeating cycles of the cosmos serve as a persistent reference to ground our thoughts and actions. These constants have maintained their stability despite major discoveries of science. Even after the momentous shift from a geocentric to a heliocentric universe, the sun still rises in the east, sets in the west, and regulates the daily and seasonal cycles that guide the rituals of our everyday existence. We now know much more about gravity, but we have yet to devise an escape from its constant presence. The advances in scientific knowledge are indeed impressive, and yet the cumulative results of this knowledge have not been able to provide an explanation of the world that adequately addresses human purpose. Therefore, if we grant constancy to the structures of our perception and to the repeating cycles that structure our lives, we must look elsewhere for the opportunity to reform our hypotheses. Looking within the foundation paradigms, we can investigate the thoughts and actions of humans reaching moments of crisis and making decisions about an appropriate course of action. We must realize that these decisions are reversible. If we can locate the junctures within the structure of the paradigm that articulate the relationships between the different elements, we can reveal the values responsible for this structure and then hypothesize other possibilities. This is the course of action that Vitruvius recommended when he addressed the problem of rebuilding Augustan Rome. The advice remains potent today.

Beginning with the clearing, we are immediately confronted with the central problem of the myth as it applies to our present condition. Vitruvius's clearing was both a literal and a metaphorical foil to the forest. His people, having left the forest in pursuit of desires whose very existence caused them to feel estranged from the natural world, needed a place to become witness to the fragile benefits of their pursuit. Although presumably independent of nature, these benefits could not be understood as autonomous. Almost without exception they would be defined in relationship to this other world. Illumination, orientation, constraint, and reason are set against the dark, limitless, and inscrutable forest. By means of analogy, metaphor, and other parallel constructions, these distinctions are extended to become the defining characteristics of our new relationship with nature. What should be obvious to us now is the crucial role played by the boundary of this clearing. This is not merely the limit to the humans' new home, it is the very means by which our thoughts and actions come into being as something recognized as distinct from the world of nature. Without the device of this edge we lack the security of knowing precisely who we are. The edge of the Vitruvian clearing brought about the first realization of spatial differentiation and the consequent valuation of spatial heterogeneity. The contrasts between clearing and forest, between known and unknown worlds, and between sacred and profane places were the essential hierarchical structures that made the world meaningful.

However, from the perspective of a world whose forests are nearly gone, the Vitruvian tale becomes vulnerable. Now our return to the clearing and the origins of dwelling reveals dimensions to the tale that prove more cautionary. The fire that created the clearing could accomplish this only as the forest was destroyed. The desire to keep the dying embers burning, as the locus around which the deliberative assembly could gather, only served to further deplete the forest and erase its presence. We notice this now because we see the results of this destruction all around us. For Vitruvius, however, the forest was without limit. His inquisitive humans could explore ever further and continue to enlarge human understanding with impunity as they expanded their reach into its unlimited depths. We should know better.

In approaching this tale again, I wish to elaborate possibilities that Vitruvius, in his forested context, found no need to pursue. Vitruvius imagined the center of his clearing marked by the dying embers of the fire. His words are ironically prophetic. For as his heroes gathered to constitute their world, they gathered around the device that literally was to be instrumental in the slow destruction of the forest. Metaphorically the fire would cause the erasure of a distinction, maintained through persistent struggle, that was fundamental to the human condition.

If we accept the validity of paradigmatic structure, however, we are not obligated to maintain the particular contingencies that have been given order by the paradigm. In fact, we must continually revisit these structures in order to confirm how they conform to our present purposes and understanding of the world. This unlimited capacity to create hypotheses about our selves and our world is one of the most remarkable conditions of being human.

We might wonder, then, how differently this tale would have unfolded if we were to find at its center not the dying embers of the fire but, instead, the living presence of a vital forest whose capacity for self-renewal promised to maintain the crucial distinction between the world of nature and human artifice. Paradigmatically at the center, the gathering around the forest would frame the potential relationship between human and nature in a substantially different way. Existing in this privileged place, the forest, like the fire, would become a locus of civic responsibility. Like the fire, it would be expected to be maintained and protected in order to participate in the initiation of speech, political structure, and architecture that are critical to making the world. But maintenance falls short of the problem as we now understand it. By the mid-eighteenth century, with deforestation well advanced, Vico still believed that within the natural cycles of growth, decay, and re-growth the forest would regenerate itself out of the decay of civilization.[1] We now know that this regeneration will require significant attention on our part. This raises important questions about the meaning of a natural world that must receive attention from humans in order to recover its former resilience.

A further consequence of our paradigmatic inversion would be to shift our valuative attention from the object or figure at the center to the more implicitly extensive ground of the forest. In other words, by locating the forest at the heart of our existence we would have placed there something that cannot be reduced to the singular presence of an independent and autonomous figure. Unlike the fire, the forest is a vital force that is pervasive, extensive, and composed of interdependent parts. Historically, we have been unimpressed with the virtues of the background texture of the world from which the apparently more interesting figure emerges to take its stand. This background is most often imagined as being empty. The consequence of this learned innocence is an almost terminal insensitivity to the rich subtleties of the teeming wild, the variegated forms and material of the landscape, the nuanced patterns of urban texture, and the rituals of the everyday. An elevation of the background does not imply a diminution of the figure. Rather it requires the enlargement of its own important compositional, metaphorical, and anthropological manifestations. With the forest at center, we will face a challenge. The human mind will be compelled to imagine figural structures to describe this strange new condition. Thus we will find at center the simultaneous presence of two constructs (figure and ground) in place of the more autonomous singular figure. This suggests a more challenging role for the reconstituted figure. It must hold its own place in the world while concurrently engaging in connections with the larger and more extensive network of relationships that characterizes the ground. Its reconsidered boundaries will need the assurance and the ambiguity that will allow our diverse and multiple civic realms to coexist and once again be held to individual responsibility. Perhaps the challenge is similar to that of the first clearing, where within the vast forest a very small figure stood out as the origin of such an immense project.

As can be seen, this is not a naive return. We bring two thousand years of history along with us. For this reason alone, the complex possibilities of this reconstitution of the origins of dwelling will generate questions sufficient to help launch the next century. Of course this history itself now becomes vulnerable much like Vitruvius's tale. Our paradigmatic inversion will prompt us to revisit all of our past and will cause us to see additional possibilities within this past that will further enlarge the understanding of our more inclusive world.

As we now return to our problematic present we might look with renewed interest at our dysfunctional cities and sprawling consumption of the earth. The models proposed as remedies to this have generally failed. I believe they have been so ineffective because they never questioned the critical relationships within the most important paradigm of all: the relationship of the center and its limits and the parallel relationship between the clearing and the forest.

Even amidst all of the pessimism that is so currently fashionable, I find it hard to resist imagining just what our world could be like in the next two millennia if the myth of origin we were to tell today did not proceed from the dying embers of a consuming fire, but instead engaged the complex and perhaps strange animating power of the forest as a more valued part of our paradigms.

Notes

1 The Origin of Dwelling

1. Marcus Vitruvius Pollio, *The Ten Books on Architecture,* trans. Morris Hicky Morgan (Cambridge: Harvard University Press, 1914), 3. My primary source for Vitruvius is the Morgan translation. The translation by Frank Granger (London: Heinemann, 1931) has much to commend, especially his inclusion of the Latin text, his scholarly notes on word usage, and the setting out of the historical context within which to understand his translation. While Granger would seem to be the preferable translation for technical and historical matters, his presentation of the mythical anecdotes underplays the poetic character that gives the Morgan edition such interest. Of course the issue of accuracy is a slippery one. Our only knowledge of the original text comes from copies written by hand at a considerable historical remove and quite likely to have accumulated a degree of contextual prejudice. My concern then is not so much for the impossible goal of a textual concordance with the precise words that Vitruvius might have written but with the layers of accumulated meanings that have been accreting around this text.

2. Vitruvius, *The Ten Books,* 38–39. The passages that accompany the illustrations at the opening of my chapters are quoted from pp. 38–40 of this edition.

3. See Hannah Arendt, *The Human Condition* (Chicago: University of Chicago Press, 1958), 7–8.

4. "The process of language formation shows for example how the chaos of immediate impressions takes on order and clarity for us only when we 'name' it and so permeate it with the function of linguistic thought and expression. . . . Thus language becomes one of the human spirit's basic implements, by which we progress from the world of mere sensation to the world of intuition and ideas." Ernst Cassirer, *The Philosophy of Symbolic Forms,* trans. Ralph Manheim, 4 vols. (New Haven: Yale University Press, 1955), 1:87–88. "Just as the particular sound mediates between the object and the man, so the whole language mediates between him and the nature that works upon him from within and without. He surrounds himself with a world of sounds in order to assimilate and elaborate the world of objects." Wilhelm von Humboldt, quoted in ibid., 2:92.

5. "Only speech enables man to be the living being he is as man. It is as one who speaks that man is-man." Martin Heidegger paraphrasing von Humboldt in "Language," in *Poetry, Language, Thought,* trans. Albert Hofstadter (New York: Harper and Row, 1971), 189.

6. Cassirer is explicit on this matter. "The function of language is not merely to repeat definitions and distinctions which are already present in the mind, but to formulate them and make them intelligible as such." Cassirer, *Philosophy of Symbolic Forms,* 1:107.

7. From his study of language and his observation that even in the most diverse languages certain spatial specifications are almost always designated by the same sounds, Cassirer concludes that language formation is the basis of our systematic articulation of spatial intuitions. "The differentiation of locations in space starts from the situation of the speaker and spreads in concentric circles until the objective whole . . . has been articulated. . . . Once he has formed a distinct representation of his own body, once he has apprehended it as a self-enclosed and intrinsically articulated organism, it becomes . . . a model according to which he constructs the world as a whole." Cassirer, *Philosophy of Symbolic Forms,* 2:206. For a thorough treatment of the relationship between language, space, and the human figure see Cassirer, "The Expression of Space and Spatial Relations," in the same volume.

8. It is necessary to understand myth not as fable, fiction, or illusion but rather in its original sense as that which is the most real. In this sense myth, unlike history with its necessary intellectual detachment from matters in the present, is a living presence supplying models for human behavior and, by that very fact, giving meaning and value to life. "It is the eternal present of the mythical event that makes possible the profane duration of historical events." Mircea Eliade, *The Sacred and the Profane,* trans. Willard R. Trask (New York: Harcourt, Brace and World, 1959), 89. See also Mircea Eliade, *Myth and Reality,* trans. Willard R. Trask (New York: Harper and Row, 1963), 2.
    "Studied alive, myth . . . is not an explanation in satisfaction of a scientific interest, but a narrative resurrection of a primeval reality, told in satisfaction of deep religious wants, moral cravings, social submissions, assertions, even practical requirements. . . . It expresses, enhances, and codifies belief; it safeguards and enforces morality; it vouches for the efficiency of ritual and contains practical rules for the guidance of man. Myth is thus a vital ingredient of human civilization; it is not an idle tale, but a hard-worked active force; it is not an intellectual explanation or an artistic imagery, but a pragmatic charter of primitive faith and moral wisdom. . . . These stories . . . are to the natives a statement of a primeval, greater, and more relevant reality, by which the present life, fates and activities of mankind are determined, the knowledge of which supplies man with the motive for the ritual and moral actions, as well as with indications as to how to perform them." B. Malinowski, *Myth in Primitive Psychology* (1926); reprinted in *Magic, Science and Religion* (New York: Doubleday, 1955), 101, 108, quoted in Eliade, *Myth and Reality,* 20.
    Although Eliade has based his work on an understanding of primitive religious societies, he warns that modern profane man, being descended from religious man, cannot erase his own history. Eliade views the modern profane world as an inheritance of the religious that is emptied of much of religion. However, even the most irreligious are not liberated from religious behavior. Eliade, *Sacred and Profane,* 201. "The

progressive de-sacralization of modern man has altered the content of his spiritual life without breaking the matrices of his imagination: a quantity of mythological litter still lingers in the ill-controlled zones of the mind." Mircea Eliade, *Images and Symbols: Studies in Religious Symbolism*, trans. Philip Mairet (New York: Sheed and Ward, 1969), 18.

9. "Myth . . . is always an account of a 'creation'; it relates how something was produced, began to be. . . . The myth is regarded as a sacred story, and hence a 'true history'. . . . The cosmogonic myth is 'true' because the existence of the world is there to prove it; the myth of the origin of death is equally true because man's mortality proves it. . . . The foremost function of myth is to reveal the exemplary models for all human rites and all significant human activities—diet or marriage, work or education, art or wisdom." Eliade, *Myth and Reality*, 6–8.

What is important within this apparent tautology is the manner in which myth relates to those things that have always concerned, and continue to concern, people directly—those events that give stability to existence primarily due to their recurring nature. To provide "exemplary models" for historical events would be antithetical to the linear passing of historical duration, but to hold the cyclical patterns of the days, seasons, or generations as merely historical robs these of the predictable repetition that gives a direct sensual structure to our lives. The myth becomes a datum to which present action can be compared in order to make further hypotheses about the outcome of our own actions in the world.

For this exemplary model to have authority it cannot be situated within the relative temporal structure of history. "What distinguishes mythical time from historical time is that for mythical time there is an absolute past which neither requires nor is susceptible of any further explanation. History dissolves being into the never-ending sequence of becoming, in which no point is singled out but every point indicates the way to one further back, so that regression into the past becomes a regressus in infinitum. . . . For myth time does not take the form of a mere relation, in which the factors of present, past, and future are persistently shifting and interchanging; here, on the contrary, a rigid barrier divides the empirical present from the mythical origin and gives to each its own inalienable character." Cassirer, *Philosophy of Symbolic Forms*, 2:106. "Myth narrates a sacred history; it relates an event that took place in primordial time, the fabled time of the 'beginnings'. . . . Myth tells how . . . a reality came into existence." Eliade, *Myth and Reality*, 5.

For a very different interpretation of time see Stephen W. Hawking, *A Brief History of Time* (New York: Bantam Books, 1988).

10. Vico sees both human institutions and language as originating in the shift from the forest to the clearing. "This was the order of human institutions: first the forests, after that the huts, then the villages, next the cities, and finally the academies. This axiom is a great principle of etymology, for this sequence of human institutions sets the pattern for the histories of words in the various native languages. Thus we observe in the Latin language that almost the whole corpus of its words had sylvan or rustic origins. For example, *lex*. First it must have meant a collection of acorns. Thence we believe is derived *ilex*, as it were *illex*, the oak (as certainly *aquilex* means collector of waters); for the oak produces the acorns by which the swine are drawn together. *Lex* was next a collection of vegetables, from which the latter were called *legumina*. Later on, at a time when vulgar letters had not yet been invented for writing down the laws, *lex* by a

necessity of civil nature must have meant a collection of citizens, or the public parliament; so that the presence of the people was the *lex,* or 'law,' that solemnized the wills that were made *calatis comitiis,* in the presence of the assembled *comitia.* Finally, collecting letters, and making, as it were, a sheaf of them for each word, was called *legere,* reading." Giambattista Vico, *The New Science of Giambattista Vico,* trans. Thomas Goddard Bergin and Max Harold Fisch, rev. ed. (Ithaca: Cornell University Press, 1968), 78.

Heidegger presents a nearly parallel description of the movement from the naming of things to questions of being, and also situates this within the clearing. "Language, by naming beings for the first time, first brings beings to word and to appearance. Only this naming nominates beings to their being from out of their being. Such saying is a projecting of the clearing, in which announcement is made of what it is that beings come into the Open as." Heidegger, "The Origin of the Work of Art," in *Poetry, Language, Thought,* 73.

The connection between the clearing and the formation of language is seen, as well, in the writing of Sedlmayr, except that for him the quality of place that Vico defines as the clearing now is the earth itself viewed as a quite specific and grounded place. Sedlmayr argues that "speech and earth are one . . . a work of poetry grows out of the earth." He dismisses synthetic inventions such as Esperanto as a rootless language. Hans Sedlmayr, *Art in Crisis,* trans. Brian Battershaw (Chicago: Henry Regnery, 1958), 150.

The meanings that converge on the word *plot* which refers both to a piece of cultivated land and the plan of a literary work, would seem to support Sedlmayr's thesis. See *Oxford English Dictionary,* 2d ed. (Oxford: Clarendon Press, 1989) s.v. "plot."

11. "No human life, not even the life of the hermit in nature's wilderness, is possible without a world which directly or indirectly testifies to the presence of other human beings. . . . All human activities are conditioned by the fact that men live together, but it is only action that cannot even be imagined outside the society of men." Arendt, *Human Condition,* 22.

Within the clearing that Vitruvius describes, both action and representation become essential characteristics of the human being's desire to create the world. Although distinct, these differing ways of being in the world converge in the artifact. "To live together in the world means essentially that a world of things is between those who have it in common, as a table is located between those who sit around it; the world, like every in-between, relates and separates men at the same time." Ibid., 52.

A thing, however, must be understood as much more than an inert object emptied of any capability to engage both human and world. "A thing, as everyone thinks he knows, is that around which the properties have assembled. We speak in this connection of the core of things. The Greeks are supposed to have called it *to hupokeimenon.* For them, this core of the thing was something lying at the ground of the thing, something always already there. The characteristics, however, are called *ta sumbebekota,* that which has always turned up already along with the given core and occurs along with it." Heidegger, "Origin of the Work of Art," 22–23.

"The Old High German word *thing* means a gathering, and specifically a gathering to deliberate on a matter under discussion, a contested matter. In consequence, the Old German words *thing* and *dinc* become the names for an affair or matter of pertinence. They denote anything that in any way bears upon men, concerns them, and that accordingly is a matter for discourse. The Romans called a matter for discourse *res.* The Greek *eiro* (*rhetos, rhetra, rhema*) means to speak about something, to deliberate on it. *Res publica* means, not the state, but that which, known to everyone, concerns everybody and is therefore deliberated in public." Heidegger, "The Thing," in *Poetry, Language, Thought,* 174. Heidegger completes the full set of connections by extending this relationship to the earth itself. "House and table join mortals to the earth." Heidegger, "Language," 199.

Heidegger's writing on the significance of the work of art can be seen as parallel to his description of the thing. In this regard his observation "To be a work is to set up a world" underscores all of the meanings that converge on the making of things. Heidegger, "Origin of the Work of Art," 44.

12. In his seminal essay on representation, Gombrich speculates on what is necessary to turn a stick hobby horse into a representation of a horse. He establishes two conditions that this stick must fulfill: "First, that its form made it just possible to ride on it; secondly—and perhaps decisively—that riding mattered." Gombrich's analysis is crucial to the idea of the engaged participant. The degree to which his first condition can be abstracted from the actual horse will depend on the intensity of his second condition. In other words, the relationship between stick and beholder is one that proceeds in both directions and consequently reveals as much about the spectator as it does about either stick or horse. E. H. Gombrich, "Meditations on a Hobby Horse," in Morris Philipson, ed., *Aesthetics Today* (Cleveland: World Publishing, 1961), 121.

13. Although the Vitruvian clearing could only be considered a primitive version of the paradisal garden, the similarities of intent and structure are revealing. Both are circumscribed by a definite boundary (Paradise being a transliteration of the Old Persian word *pairidaeza,* referring to a walled garden), and both are defined by a center occupied by some form of nature, either the fire in Vitruvius, or a fountain or tree. The actual division of the garden in the Persian examples into a quadripartite representation of cosmic orientation, however, is only hinted at in Vitruvius. It is instructive to compare the purpose directly ascribed to the Paradise garden with those only implied in the Vitruvian myth. "The idea of Paradise as a garden is one of man's oldest ideals. Since the beginning of history, most probably in prehistory, societies which had nothing else in common shared the concept of Paradise as the ideal garden, a secure and everlasting garden. Almost universal in human experience, this concept of Paradise in which man transcends his frail human condition, has persisted while many of the civilizations which adhered to it have disappeared. Belief in the myth has lessened the pain of life and fear of death. The image of a place of perfect and eternal peace and plenty can make a difficult temporal existence meaningful and its transitory nature acceptable." Elizabeth B. Moynihan, *Paradise as a Garden* (New York: George Braziller, 1979), 2. Or, "We may thus discover in gardens models of the way in which the mind conceives its relation to the world external to itself. . . . They become arenas in which the externality of the world is at least temporarily overcome" Terry Comito, *The Idea of the Garden in the Renaissance* (New Brunswick: Rutgers University Press, 1978), xii. "This sense of enclosure is not the accidental result of the Fall, but part of Eden's essential nature. As Milton knew, it is the fallen world that is a 'fenceless' one. . . . In Eden man discovered rather than brought those influences which were important and . . . what he discovered was a reality which defined his own being" (ibid., 34, 39).

It seems obvious that paradise cannot exist independent of the forest, which is both the context from which this place is distinguished and a place in its own right. Together, these constitute a complete world. Bachelard supports this observation when he describes the forest as almost precisely opposed to paradise, characterizing it as a limitless world (without the boundary crucial to paradise) where orientation is impossible. Gaston Bachelard, *The Poetics of Space*, trans. Maria Jolas (Boston: Beacon Press, 1964), 185.

Eliade defines the nostalgia for paradise as "the desire to find oneself always and without effort at the center of the world, at the heart of reality." Eliade, *Images and Symbols*, 55. See also his *Myths, Dreams, and Mysteries* (New York: Harper and Row, 1960), 59, where Eliade explains the paradisiac myth as a transcendence of the profane time of history in order to achieve a sense of immortality. Thus in the structure of the paradisal garden the ideal, formal patterns relate to either the enduring presence of solar orientation or the marking of life through cyclical rather than linear patterns of time.

McClung captures the paradoxical quality of this state of being that is also able to have a concrete manifestation: "Paradise, in all senses of the word, is the most striking place I can discover where an immaterial vision and a material structure or system of relationships are brought together and depend upon each other. . . . The search for Paradise is thus an effort to discover the correct relationship between man, nature, and craft." William A. McClung, *The Architecture of Paradise* (Berkeley: University of California Press, 1983), 1–2.

14. To see how the circle became a form of primary significance during the Renaissance, see Leon Battista Alberti, *On the Art of Building in Ten Books*, trans. Joseph Rykwert, Neil Leach, and Robert Tavernor (Cambridge: MIT Press, 1988), book 9, chapter 4. Also Rudolf Wittkower, "The Centrally Planned Church and the Renaissance," in *Architectural Principles in the Age of Humanism*, 3d ed. (London: Alec Tiranti, 1967).

15. These primitive people gathered about the fire also define a field within the clearing in a manner described by Rudolf Schwarz: "The people are bound hand in hand into the ring but they are not completely absorbed by it. Their eyes remain free, turned toward the circle's inner field: life passes out through their eyes and returns through them, now laden with world. Thus the whole field within the ring is looked across and, as it were, lived through. This field becomes a second element of the plan. Standing in the ring the people mark off a bit of land as the secure earth of home; a city is found and fortified by an encircling wall. . . . The ring becomes the form of cohesion, of girdling, of embrace. It becomes the expression of abundance and safety. Since of all the figures, the ring unites the smallest perimeter with the largest content, it is the richest and the most indwelling of them all. This is again connected with its stability, for at the perimeter the eccentric pressure of the contents is transformed into tension and it is against this tension that the ring establishes its inviolability. And so it can be said that the abundance of the inner field is transformed into the inviolability of the binding ring. . . . In the ring everyone may look at everyone else—here in the small circle is utter unreserve, the openness of all to all. If the lines of all these possible encounters are drawn, a network is formed, spanned between the people. This network is the elemental form of social life and hence above all else it is the form of spoken intercourse, of speech. . . . The eyes . . . gather together in the altar, in the point which all eyes share. . . . In it, the people are united . . . and each person [knows] that the true way to what lies within, into the other's heart, passes through the center." Rudolf Schwarz, *The Church Incarnate* (1938), trans. Cynthia Harris (Chicago: Henry Regnery, 1958), 40–42.

16. The forest is a complex phenomenon, at once revered for its resources and feared for the darkness that obscures the human's necessary relationship to the sky and confounds orientation. J. B. Jackson is one of few contemporary authors to capture the ambiguities of the forest. "The perpetual challenge of the forest stirred the imagination as did no other feature in the environment. It was the forest where the outlaw went to hide; it was there that adventurous men went to make a new farm and a new and freer life. It teemed with wolves, boars, bears and wild oxen. It contained in its depths the abandoned clearings and crumbling ruins of an earlier civilization. It was a place of terror to the farmer and at the same time a place of refuge. He was obliged to enter it for wood and game and in search of pasture. For hundreds of years the forest determined the spread of population and represented the largest source of raw materials; it was an outlet for every energy. Its dangers as well as its wealth became part of the daily existence of every man and woman." J. B. Jackson, "Ghosts at the Door," in Ervin H. Zube and Margaret J. Zube, eds., *Changing Rural Landscapes* (Amherst: University of Massachusetts Press, 1977).

Other contemporary texts that have developed this theme include Leo Marx, *The Machine in the Garden* (New York: Oxford University Press, 1964), and the brilliant work of Robert Pogue Harrison, *Forests: The Shadow of Civilization* (Chicago: University of Chicago Press, 1992).

17. Vitruvius seems unwilling to make a clear distinction and consequent separation between the house as a private retreat and the public activity of gathering that occurs within the clearing. Rather than seeing this as a problem, I think it shows an intense interrelationship between these two modes of existence, as against our contemporary situation where the dwelling is rarely considered relevant to public life and public life has little influence on the life and form of the dwelling. It is notable that many of the names for public institutions (court house, town hall, house of god, house of representatives, etc.) show a grounding in the house. In this regard, I will heed Bachelard's advice concerning the house: "The house is one of the greatest powers of integration for the thoughts, memories and dreams of mankind. . . . In the life of a man, the house thrusts aside contingencies, its councils of continuity are unceasing. Without it, man would be a dispersed being . . . it is the human being's first world." Bachelard, *Poetics of Space*, 6, 7. Thus, it is possible to extend Alberti's analogy between house and city to show how both are constructs that reflect a comprehensive and engaged understanding of the world. Alberti, *Art of Building*, book 1, chapter 6.

Arendt sees that the privacy of the house ultimately makes public life legitimate. "A life spent entirely in public, in the presence of others, becomes, as we would say, shallow. While it retains its visibility, it loses the quality of rising into sight from some darker ground which must remain hidden if it is not to lose its depth in a very real, non-objective sense. The only efficient way to guarantee the darkness of what needs to be hidden against the light of publicity is private property, a privately owned place to hide in." Arendt, *Human Condition*, 71.

18. "Purpose has no place in biology, but history has no meaning without it." George Kubler, *The Shape of Time* (New Haven: Yale University Press, 1962), 8.

19. "Language is never primarily the expression of thinking, feeling, and willing. Language is the primal dimension within which man's essence is first able to correspond at all to Being and its claim, and, in corresponding, to belong to Being. This primal

corresponding, expressly carried out, is thinking. Through thinking, we first learn to dwell in the realm in which there comes to pass the restorative surmounting of the destining of Being, the surmounting of Enframing." Martin Heidegger, *The Question Concerning Technology and Other Essays,* trans. William Lovitt (New York: Harper and Row, 1977), 41.

Although somewhat opaque, Heidegger's argument is that it is through language that the mind is able to grasp and hold onto the structural relationships that allow for any orientation in the world. For Heidegger, orientation is the initial step in locating a place in the world and therefore the first step in dwelling.

20. The most profound analysis of the political basis of architecture in recent times is found in Carroll William Westfall, "Politics," in Robert Jan Van Pelt and Carroll William Westfall, *Architectural Principles in the Age of Historicism* (New Haven: Yale University Press, 1991).

21. For further elaboration of the "simple contemplation of the celestial vault" see Eliade, *Sacred and Profane,* 118.

22. Vico understood that the world of the human being was a construct derived from the unique properties of the human will that could frame and act on an intention rather than merely react to natural circumstances. Consequently he advised that it was this structure of thought and action that must be examined for the most profound understanding of the world; an attempt to understand the origins of humankind should seek "its proofs not in the external world but within the modifications of the mind who mediates it. For since this world of notions has certainly been made by men, it is within these modifications that its principles should have been sought." Vico, *New Science,* 374. "But in the night of thick darkness enveloping the earliest antiquity, so remote from ourselves, there shines the eternal and never failing light of truth beyond all question: that the world of civil society has certainly been made by men, and that its principles are therefore to be found within the modifications of our own human mind" (331).

23. "Just as the universe unfolds from a center and stretches out toward the four cardinal points, the village comes into existence around an intersection." Eliade, *Sacred and Profane,* 45.

2 Paradigmatic Structures

1. "The archaic world knows nothing of 'profane' activities: every act which has a definite meaning—hunting, fishing, agriculture; games, conflicts, sexuality,—in some way participates in the sacred. . . . The only profane activities are those which have no mythical meaning, that is, which lack exemplary models." Mircea Eliade, *The Myth of the Eternal Return,* trans. Willard R. Trask (Princeton: Princeton University Press, 1954), 27–28. Elsewhere, Eliade emphasizes how, in the absence of paradigms, a world can never come into existence: "For in the view of archaic societies everything that is not 'our world' is not yet a world." Mircea Eliade, *The Sacred and the Profane,* trans. Willard R. Trask (New York: Harcourt, Brace and World, 1949), 32.

Norberg-Schulz sees this same activity as the basis for any culture: "From birth on we try to orientate ourselves in the environment and establish a certain order. A common order is called culture. . . . Participation in a culture means that one knows how to use its common symbols. The culture integrates the single personality in an ordered world based upon meaningful interactions." Christian Norberg-Schulz, "Meaning in Architecture," in Charles Jencks and George Baird, eds., *Meaning in Architecture* (New York: George Braziller, 1969), 220.

2. My interest in beginnings was catalyzed by Edward Said, who defined beginning as "the first step in the intentional production of meaning" and qualified intention as "a notion that includes everything that later develops out of it." Edward W. Said, *Beginnings* (Baltimore: Johns Hopkins University Press, 1975), 5, 12. See also Heidegger: "The beginning already contains the end latent within itself.... The beginning ... always contains the undisclosed abundance of the unfamiliar and extraordinary, which means that it also contains strife with the familiar and ordinary." Martin Heidegger, "The Origin of the Work of Art," in *Poetry, Language, Thought,* trans. Albert Hofstadter (New York: Harper and Row, 1971), 77.

3. A survey of these difficulties can be found in an amusing entry by Peter Heath in Paul Edwards, ed., *The Encyclopedia of Philosophy,* 8 vols. (New York: Macmillan, 1967), s.v. "nothing."

4. "According to the opening Prologue of the Gospel of St. John, in the beginning the Word was with God. The attempt is made not only to free the question of origin from the fetters of a rational-logical explanation, but also to set aside the limits of a merely logical description of language." Martin Heidegger, "Language," in *Poetry, Language, Thought,* 193.

5. "Therefore, in the realm of thinking, a painstaking effort to think through still more primally what was primally thought is not the absurd wish to revive what is past, but rather the sober readiness to be astounded before the coming of what is early." Martin Heidegger, *The Question Concerning Technology and Other Essays,* trans. William Lovitt (New York: Harper and Row, 1977), 22.

6. Noting the Jewish tradition that God gave man a secret—how to start anew—Van Pelt quotes Elie Wiesel's commentary on the new beginning made by Adam and Eve after their exile from paradise: "It is not given to man to begin. Beginning is God's privilege. But it is given to man to begin again—and he does so every time he chooses to defy death and side with the living." In Robert Jan Van Pelt and Carroll William Westfall, *Architectural Principles in the Age of Historicism* (New Haven: Yale University Press, 1991), 323.

Arendt equates action itself with beginning and argues that the ability to initiate action gives to the human a degree of freedom that the animal can never posses. "To act ... means to take an initiative, to begin.... This beginning is not the same as the beginning of the world; it is not the beginning of something but of somebody, who is a beginner himself. With the creation of man, the principle of beginning came into the world itself, which, of course, is only another way of saying that the principle of freedom was created when man was created but not before." Hannah Arendt, *The Human Condition* (Chicago: University of Chicago Press, 1958), 177.

See also Van Pelt's citing of Kierkegaard's distinction between recollection and repetition: "The dialectic of repetition is easy, for that which is repeated has been—otherwise it could not be repeated—but the very fact that it has been makes the repetition into something new. When the Greeks said that all knowing is recollecting, they said that all existence, which is, has been; when one says that life is a repetition, one says: actuality, which has been, now comes into existence." Van Pelt and Westfall, *Architectural Principles,* 242–245.

Cassirer, in his discussion on repetition, shows the relationship between what is being repeated and our memory of it: "In order to remember a content, consciousness must previously have possessed itself of that content in a way differing from mere sensation or perception. The mere repetition of the given at another time does not suffice; in this repetition a new kind of conception and formation must be manifested. For every 'reproduction' of a content embodies a new level of 'reflection'." Ernst Cassirer, *The Philosophy of Symbolic Forms,* trans. Ralph Manheim, 4 vols. (New Haven: Yale University Press, 1955), 1:90.

7. Edward Said maintains that a beginning represents a discontinuity with what precedes it, yet he acknowledges the difficulty of beginning with a wholly new start: "God himself does not begin completely from nothing. Noah and the ark comprise a piece of the old world initiating the new world." Said, *Beginnings,* 34.

8. "If the world is to be lived in, it must be founded—and no world can come into birth in the chaos of the homogeneity and relativity of profane space." Eliade, *Sacred and Profane,* 22. Eliade extends this observation and shows that the sacred space that is constituted as part of this founding, and is located within the structure of myth itself, has certain predictable patterns of order that connect the human being to the world. I will discuss this further in the fourth chapter.

9. It is useful to comment on some of the fundamental properties of symbolic imagination that are suggested by this story.

"Man's conquest of the world undoubtedly rests on the supreme development of his brain, which allows him to synthesize, delay, and modify his reactions by the interpolation of symbols in the gaps and confusions of direct experience, and by means of 'verbal signs' to add the experience of other people to his own." Susanne Langer, *Philosophy in a New Key* (New York: Mentor Books, 1948), 22. In Langer's later writing (see *Feeling and Form*) she includes the whole range of nondiscursive structures within her understanding of symbolic thought. Important here is, first, the position of the symbol between the human and the world of the senses and, second, the inclusive, cumulative, and public nature of the symbol.

Through this public intermediary position the symbol becomes a complex and ambiguous construct. It mostly lacks the conventional attribution of meaning that is necessary to the efficient functioning of the sign, yet its ability to suggest complex, inclusive, open worlds renders it invaluable as the essential component of synthetic thinking. The symbol achieves its greatest expressive capacity and is able to take on an inclusive range of possibilities precisely as it becomes the least explicit about its intentions. It is therefore crucial that the symbol not be mistaken for a sign, which signals its purpose in as unambiguous a manner as possible. The difficulty of the symbol, then, is that while it is in itself incomplete and suggestive, what it suggests is a hypothesis about the world that by definition and intention must be complete and whole. An understanding of this quality is essential to the intentional making of the symbol, and will be discussed further in the third chapter. Langer similarly observes: "Symbols are not proxy for their objects, but are vehicles for the conception of objects." Langer, *Philosophy in a New Key,* 49.

It is possible to extract a parallel argument from Aristotle's theories of poetic imitation and his conception of the purposes of tragedy, of which he says: "Tragedy, then, is an imitation of an action that is serious, complete, and of a certain magnitude." S. H. Butcher, *Aristotle's Theory of Poetry and Fine Art,* 4th ed. (New York: Dover, 1951), *Poetics,* v.1, 2; all further quotations of Aristotle are from the Butcher translation. It is notable not only that the themes of tragedy are serious but that they require closure. Implicit in this description is the need for particular human actions to lead to predictable and repeatable conclusions, thus functioning as reliable guides by which individuals can measure their own intentions. See also Eliade's discussion of images, where he explains that "to have imagination is to be able to see the world in its totality." Mircea Eliade, *Images and Symbols: Studies in Religious Symbolism,* trans. Philip Mairet (New York: Sheed and Ward, 1969), 20.

Frye relates symbolic thinking in literature to ritual and thus grounds this thinking in the repetitive structures of action that seek to explain the world by imitating its cyclical patterns: "The narrative aspect of literature is a recurrent act of symbolic communication: in other words a ritual. Narrative is studied by the archetypal critic as ritual or imitation of human action as a whole, and not simply as a *mimesis praxeos* or imitation of an action." Northrop Frye, *Anatomy of Criticism: Four Essays* (Princeton: Princeton University Press, 1957), 104–105.

Although the symbol most effectively gathers the many conflicting meanings of a complex world when it is the least circumscribed, it would immediately collapse into chaotic relativity if it were not held together by its own internal structure. Frye describes this condition in the context of literary criticism: "Criticism as knowledge, the criticism which is compelled to keep on talking about the subject, recognizes the fact that there is a center of the order of words. Unless there is such a center, there is nothing to prevent the analogies supplied by convention and genre from being an endless series of free associations, perhaps suggestive, perhaps even tantalizing, but never creating a real structure. The study of archetypes is the study of literary symbols as parts of a whole. . . . We spoke before of the mythical view of literature as leading to the conception of an order or nature as a whole being imitated by a corresponding order of words." Ibid., 116–117.

Mircea Eliade's research in the structure of myths and their significance within primitive cultures has been important as a reaction against nineteenth-century positivism, showing that it is still possible for the symbol to act as one of the most remarkable instruments of knowledge. See especially Eliade, *Images and Symbols,* 9.

10. To a considerable degree the ideas of paradigmatic structure overlap those of typology. I have deliberately avoided this more familiar term since its presence has such a strong and disruptive effect on architectural discourse. Typology has recently become one of those "polarizing issues," to use Gombrich's term whose mere presence serves to split discourse into a contrived confrontation incapable of resolution. See E. H. Gombrich, "The Logic of Vanity Fair: Alternatives to Historicism in the Study of Fashions, Style and Taste," in Paul Schilpp, ed., *The Philosophy of Karl Popper* (La Salle, Ill.: Open Court, 1974).

It is not surprising, however, that typology arouses such emotion. At stake is whether human thought and action are autonomous or are conditioned by factors intrinsic to the structure of the human being and the context within which it operates. At least partially due to the shift from religious belief to scientific empiricism and the coincident rise in the valuation of an independent will, perceived limits to free inquiry will necessarily be met with increasing hostility. This hostility is, unfortunately, directed toward typology. It is commonly believed that a reliance on type can come only with significant compromise to artistic invention, making the solution to new problems ineffective. Yet it offers something equally vital, the larger mediating structure essential to promote communication and agreement. This is especially true within architecture. The architect, no longer a functioning part of a comprehensive mythic, religious, or even political structure, is left only with the constantly changing empirical instrumentality of technology or the anxious search for authority in personal expression. But a reexamination of the reasoning in several seminal texts on typology suggests a way to reframe the problem so that other conclusions are possible.

Laugier, in his *Essay on Architecture*, hoped to counter the willful excesses in personal expression that he felt characterized the Baroque by establishing architectural authority on principles derived from nature. In the mid-eighteenth century, however, nature was valued more for its processes of growth and form than as the ineffable ideal of the early Renaissance. Laugier's mythic account of the primitive hut gives precedence to nature's ability to solve the immediate problems of physical shelter, rather than to its ability to act as a more comprehensive model for the human's world. It comes as little surprise that this instrumental valuation of nature leads to his most visible contribution to the typological argument—his drawing of a specific hut. Presented in this way, there was no doubt that this artifact was meant to guide quite literally all further architectural criticism and production. Although Laugier always referred to this hut as a model, his insistence that this model act as the "simple principle" for all subsequent rules gives it a role much closer to that of the type. The legitimacy of this elevation of the thing to an idea has been further reinforced by Joseph Rykwert's unexpected substitution of Laugier's word *modèle* for *type* in his translation of this passage in his influential book *On Adam's House in Paradise* (New York: Museum of Modern Art, 1972). See also Marc-Antoine Laugier, *An Essay on Architecture*, trans. Wolfgang Herrmann and Anni Herrmann (Los Angeles: Hennessey and Ingalls, 1977).

Of all the modern writers on typology, Quatremère de Quincy approaches most closely Aristotle's ideas of imitation, which distinguish between the idea of a thing and its material manifestation. This is demonstrated in his admonition to those who fail to understand the difference between type and model: "They confound the idea of type (the original reason of the thing), which can neither command nor furnish the motif or the means of an exact likeness, with the idea of the model (the complete thing) which is bound to a formal resemblance." Antoine Chrysostome Quatremère de Quincy, "Type," in *Encyclopédie Méthodique, Architecture*, vol. 3, pt. II (Paris, 1825), quoted in translation in Anthony Vidler, "The Idea of Type," *Oppositions* 8 (1977). Quatremère understood type to be the essence or "germ" from which all further development is to be guided. But when he comes closest to defining that essence, it splits into three (cave, hut, tent)— "these three states of natural life, the origin of every type of construction associated with all people"—and we are left to conclude that these quite particular contingent responses to differing local environmental conditions, things we would have expected to be called models, have slipped into the category of type. Quatremère, quoted in Sylvia Lavin, *Quatremère de Quincy and the Invention of a Modern Language of Architecture* (Cambridge: MIT Press, 1992), 21.

J. N. L. Durand is perhaps the most vilified of those proposing a typological basis for architecture. In his *Précis des leçons d'architecture* (1819; rpt. Nordlingen: Verlag Dr. Alfons Uhl, 1981), he elevates the grid from an idea about the homogeneity of space to near iconic status as a thing upon which to base the assembly of his kit of neoclassical pieces. He thus erases an even earlier valuation of the grid as a representation of the ideal correspondence between sacred and worldly order. Even a writer as astute as Argan in his excellent article on the modern revival of interest in typology, where he argues for Quatremère's notion of the vagueness of type as it is an essence or idea of a thing, concludes with reference to "new" types necessitated by changes in industrial production. As a consequence, he mistakenly endows what could only be a model responsive to contingent change (an artifact) with the capability of a type. Giulio Carlo Argan, "On the Typology of Architecture," trans. Joseph Rykwert, *Architectural Design* 33 (1963). Of course Pevsner's *A History of Building Types,* which classifies historical building examples according to program, needs little comment.

This predilection for finding transcendent authority within the ephemerality and historicity of a thing can never succeed. But to abandon the typological project for this reason is to misunderstand its most profound intention: the desire to find a structure that gathers the things of the world into a comprehensible whole and gives a known place to things and actions that otherwise would be adrift. This is a synthetic way of thinking. We are making hypotheses about relationships among pieces not previously thought to share anything of substance. These pieces take on value not so much from their ability to remain distinct and different from all that surrounds them but from their differing ability to reveal the possibility of something fundamentally similar. This possibility can actually provoke and guide the coming together of the miscellany of unrelated things we find around us to form a coherent world.

Once we acknowledge what Aristotle, and even Quatremère, knew about the futility of reducing the essence of anything to something so implausible as a thing, we can look to the structure of relationships that would follow from the hypotheses put forward in the search for typicality. Rather than finding the typological project a failure for placing limits on human imagination, we now see its results as evidence of the amazing capability of the human mind: it construes ever more elaborate structures in order to keep relating the things we make to the world we find. Although outside the scope of this text, it is interesting to think of revisiting Laugier's hut, Semper's hearths, mounds, walls, and roofs, and even Durand's grids to see what they reveal about the relationships that each proposes between the human being and the world.

See Gottfried Semper, *The Four Elements of Architecture and Other Writings,* trans. Harry Mallgrave and Wolfgang Herrmann (Cambridge: Cambridge University Press, 1989). See also the very important arguments linking type and institution in Carroll William Westfall, "Building Types," in Van Pelt and Westfall, *Architectural Principles.* For a discussion of the operation and significance of synthetic thought see Ernst Cassirer, "Particular Categories of Mythical Thinking," in *Philosophy of Symbolic Forms.*

11. Gombrich argues that all stylistic classification can be reduced to the polarity of the classical and the nonclassical, which he sees as parallel to the norm and its variations. He is not arguing for the primacy of any particular style, nor even that a style as such has an actual prescribed existence. What interests him is the possibility that style, itself emptied of its conventional meanings, could instead be seen as an instrument by which we measure human intention. Used in this way, these forms of classification allow us to

judge other achievements in the arts relative to these intentions: "There is something like an 'essence' of the classic that permits us to plot other works of art at a variable distance from this central point." E. H. Gombrich, *Norm and Form* (London: Phaidon, 1966), 96.

Vico argues likewise for the need to examine the structures of the mind by which we apprehend and act in the world. The "principles" that can be deduced from them would seem to parallel the "norm" that Gombrich describes. "The world of civil society has certainly been made by men ... its principles are therefore to be found within the modifications of our own human mind." Giambattista Vico, *The New Science of Giambattista Vico*, trans. Thomas Goddard Bergin and Max Harold Fisch, rev. ed. (Ithaca: Cornell University Press, 1968), 97.

When Le Corbusier addresses the planning of cities, he too finds it necessary to refer to the founding conditions of architecture. Here he explicitly extends one of the themes he had already introduced in his own version of the myth of origins in *Towards a New Architecture*. "Placed in the midst of a chaotic nature, man for his own security creates and surrounds himself with a zone of protection in harmony with what he is and what he thinks; he needs a retreat, a citadel in which he can feel secure; he needs things whose existence he has himself determined. The things he makes for himself are a creation which contrasts all the more with his natural surroundings because its aim is closer to his mind." Le Corbusier, *The City of Tomorrow*, trans. Frederick Etchells (1929; rpt. Cambridge: MIT Press, 1971), 28.

12. Quatremère writes: "In truth, the pleasure which is produced by works of imitation proceeds from the act of comparing. It is certain that the eye and the mind, whose operation is here the same, are required to judge, and, in order to judge, they must compare, deriving enjoyment only from this twofold condition." Antoine Chrysostome Quatremère de Quincy, *An Essay on the Nature, the End, and the Means of Imitation in the Fine Arts*, trans. J. C. Kent (London: Smith, Elder and Co., 1837), 14. He follows this with the logical observation that an imitation that involved an identical repetition would not give any pleasure since there would be nothing to judge or compare. The copy further "deprives the imitation or the image, of that fictious part which constitutes at once its essence and its character" (102–103). Quatremère sees the strength of imitation as being derived from this "fictious part": the freedom of expression the imitation acquires when it is no longer bound to be a faithful copy. He qualifies this "fictious part" by noting its incompleteness (121). It is this open, incomplete quality that allows abstraction to recompose with other entities to form complex structures: "We have shown that the first means for bringing about this recomposition is the exchanging the particular form and existence of things for a generalized form and existence" (358). This brings his theory of imitation in line with the writing of Langer on the qualities of the symbol (see note 9).

13. Frye uses the term "desire" to distinguish what I have been referring to as purpose from the wants associated with animal survival: "The archetypal critic studies the poem as a part of poetry, and poetry as part of the total human imitation of nature that we call civilization. Civilization is not merely an imitation of nature, but the process of making a total human form out of nature, and it is impelled by the force that we have just called desire. The desire for food and shelter is not content with roots and caves: it produces farming and architecture. Desire is thus not a simple response to need, for an animal

may need food without planting a garden to get it, nor is it a simple response to want, or desire for something in particular. It is neither limited to nor satisfied by objects, but is the energy that leads human society to develop its own form. Desire in this sense is the social aspect of what we met on the literal level as emotion, an impulse toward expression which would have remained amorphous if the poem had not liberated it by providing the form of its expression." Frye, *Anatomy of Criticism*, 105–106.

Aristotle sees the issue as our fulfillment of nature's uncompleted purposes. He brings a critical stance to this completion or "correction" of nature's failings: "There is an ideal form which is present in each individual phenomenon but imperfectly manifested. This form impresses itself as a sensuous appearance on the mind of the artist; he seeks to give it a more complete expression, to bring to light the ideal which is only half revealed in the world of reality. His distinctive work as an artist consists in stamping the given material with the impress of the form which is universal." Butcher, *Aristotle*, 153. "Imitation, so understood, is a creative act. It is the expression of the concrete thing under an image which answers to its true idea. To seize the universal, and to reproduce it in simple and sensuous form is not to reflect a reality already familiar through sense perceptions; rather it is a rivalry of nature, a completion of her unfulfilled purposes, a correction of her failures." Butcher paraphrasing Aristotle, ibid., 154.

It is interesting to see how Ozenfant similarly recognizes our apparent desire for structure in the world and proposes relationships to nature reminiscent of Aristotle. "It is one of man's passions to disentangle apparent chaos. He has to harmonise the universe to his own mental structure, and he does so by choosing from nature what fits into the working of his mind." Amédée Ozenfant, *Foundations of Modern Art*, trans. John Rodker (1931; rpt. New York: Dover, 1952), 196.

14. Qualifying the relationship between the paradigm and the world, Quatremère refers to the "ideal" and sets this off against "reality": "There [in the realm of the ideal], the artist, quitting the barren region of reality, where men, deeds, and objects present themselves only such as they are, takes his stand, and creates for us a new world, in which they are made to seem such as nature tells us they might be. There, all existences are aggrandized and ennobled, by exchanging the particular truths of imitation, for that abstract and generalized truth which comprehends the others also." Quatremère, *Essay*, 248.

Eliade explains this relationship by showing how individual occurrences or things are assimilated into categories or archetypes: "Popular memory finds difficulty in retaining individual events and real figures. The structures by means of which it functions are different: categories instead of events, archetypes instead of historical personages. The historical personage is assimilated to his mythical model (hero, etc.), while the event is identified with the category of mythical actions. . . . If certain epic poems preserve what is called 'historical truth', this truth almost never has to do with definite persons and events, but with institutions, customs, landscapes." Eliade, *Myth of the Eternal Return*, 43. Eliade sees the archaic mentality as not just uninterested but actually unwilling to accept what is individual, preserving only what is exemplary (44). This is fundamental to Aristotle: "Poetry, therefore, is a more philosophical and a higher thing than history: for poetry tends to express the universal, history the particular" (*Poetics* ix.3); or according to Butcher, "Poetry expresses the permanent possibilities of human nature, it does not merely tell the story of an individual life." Butcher, *Aristotle*, 164.

Cassirer extends these observations: "The particular must not be left to stand alone, but must be made to take its place in a context, where it appears as part of a logical structure." Cassirer, *Philosophy of Symbolic Forms*, 1:77.

Quatremère grants to the ideal the prerogative to suppress or alter the detail (the particular), yet the limits he places on possible deviations show the importance of maintaining a recoverable relation to the particular: "Still farther concessions in the details are permitted to imitation. They are termed licenses; and the word sufficiently indicates that they are only so many permissions granted to art for departing occasionally from the strictness of its rules, not in order to violate them, but the better to observe their spirit, being merely exceptions, the object of which is to aid in the fulfillment of the conditions to which it is subjected." Quatremère, *Essay*, 145–146.

15. "Every fact in history is an answer to a question and that evidence which is useful and true and sufficient in answer to question B may be false and useless in answer to question A." David Hackett Fischer, *Historians' Fallacies* (New York: Harper and Row, 1970), 62.

16. "The possession of originality cannot make an artist unconventional; it drives him further into convention, obeying the law of the art itself, which seeks constantly to reshape itself from its own depths." Frye, *Anatomy of Criticism*, 132.

17. Similarly Wölfflin writes on the impulse that drives the development of art: "The effect of picture on picture as a factor in style is much more important than what comes directly from the imitation of nature.... It is a dilettantist notion that an artist could ever take up his stand before nature without any preconceived ideas. But what he has taken over as concept of representation, and how this concept goes on working in him, is much more important than anything he takes from direct observation." Heinrich Wölfflin, *Principles of Art History*, trans. M. D. Hottinger, 7th ed. (New York: Dover, 1929), 230. Gombrich adds to this: "Contrary to the hopeful belief of many artists, the 'innocent eye' which should see the world afresh would not see it at all. It would smart under the painful impact of a chaotic medley of forms and colors." E. H. Gombrich, "Meditations on a Hobby Horse," in Morris Philipson, ed., *Aesthetics Today* (Cleveland: World Publishing, 1961), 123.

A central theme in Frye's writing on literary criticism is the strength of the preexisting literary structures or genres that provide the crucial context for the new work. "The new poem, like the new baby, is born into an already existing order of words, and is typical of the structure of poetry to which it is attached.... Literature shapes itself, and is not shaped externally; the forms of literature can no more exist outside of literature than the forms of sonata and rondo can exist outside music." Frye, *Anatomy of Criticism*, 97. "Virgil discovered, according to Pope, that following nature was ultimately the same thing as following Homer" (95–96).

The idea of paradigmatic structure can clearly be seen in Frye's concept of the genre in literary criticism. He writes that if a pattern is unique to Shakespeare, for instance, the explanation might be at least partly psychological. "But if we find it in half a dozen of his contemporaries, we clearly have to allow for convention. And if we find it in a dozen dramatists of different ages and cultures, we have to allow for genre, for the structural requirements of drama itself." Ibid., 111.

18. "Someone said: 'The dead writers are remote from us because we know so much more than they did.' Precisely, and they are what we know." T. S. Eliot, "Tradition and the Individual Talent," in *Selected Essays, 1917–1932* (London: Faber and Faber, 1961), 16.

"Whether in science or the arts, if we look for the source of an achievement we can observe that what a man does either repeats or refutes what someone else has done— repeats it in other tones, refines or amplifies or simplifies it, loads or overloads it with meaning; or else rebuts, overturns, destroys and denies it, but thereby assumes it and has invisibly used it." Paul Valéry, "Letter about Mallarmé," quoted in Said, *Beginnings*, 15.

"Art does not itself repeat itself, it prolongs itself." Léonce Rosenberg, quoted in Ozenfant, *Foundations of Modern Art*, 44.

19. *Oxford English Dictionary*, 2d ed. (Oxford: Clarendon Press, 1989), s.v. "invent."

20. Eliot, describing the obvious causality of the past on the present, turns this argument around to show how the present can unexpectedly alter the past. The past is not an absolute, fixed thing but has value primarily as it elucidates an ever-changing present; consequently, our understanding of the past and the history that records it will always be influenced by the present. "No poet, no artist of any art, has his complete meaning alone. His significance, his appreciation is the appreciation of his relation to the dead poets and artists. . . . The necessity that he shall conform, that he shall cohere, is not one sided; what happens when a new work of art is created is something that happens simultaneously to all the works of art which preceded it. The existing monuments form an ideal order among themselves, which is modified by the introduction of the new (the really new) work of art among them. The existing order is complete before the new work arrives; for order to persist after the supervention of novelty, the whole existing order must be, if ever so slightly, altered; and so the relations, proportions, values of each work of art toward the whole are readjusted; and this is conformity between the old and the new. . . . The past should be altered by the present as much as the present is directed by the past." Eliot, "Tradition and the Individual Talent," 15.

21. "Rituals cluster around the cyclical movements of the sun, the moon, the seasons, and human life. Every crucial periodicity of experience: dawn, sunset, the phases of the moon, seed-time and harvest, the equinoxes and the solstices, birth, initiation, marriage, and death, get rituals attached to them. The pull of ritual is toward pure cyclical narrative, which, if there could be such a thing, would be automatic and unconscious repetition. In the middle of all this recurrence, however, is the central recurrent cycle of sleeping and waking life, the daily frustration of the ego, the nightly awakening of a titanic self." Frye, *Anatomy of Criticism*, 105.

22. "What gives the myth an operational value is that the specific pattern described is timeless; it explains the present and the past as well as the future." Claude Lévi-Strauss, *Structural Anthropology*, trans. Claire Jacobson and Brooke Grundfest Schoepf (New York: Basic Books, 1963), 209. In Lévi-Strauss's account, myth has qualities that are similar to those of the paradigm. It is the mythic concern with the relational rather than the

historicity of the story that allows myth to be studied for its common structural themes. Lévi-Strauss's most crucial observation concerns the mistake of seeking the one true version of the myth. He proposes that myth can only be defined as consisting of all its versions. This shifts the structural analysis of myth away from the singular story toward a comparison of the differences among many stories. What then interests Lévi-Strauss is the meaning of the transformation among these versions. "A structural analysis of the myth content can . . . furnish rules of transformation which enable us to shift from one variant to another by means of operations similar to those of algebra" (235).

23. *The Random House Dictionary of the English Language,* unabridged edition (New York: Random House, 1969), s.v. "paradigm."

24. "Man is a classifying animal, and he has an incurable propensity to regard the network he has himself imposed on the variety of experience as belonging to the objective world of things." While raising this caution, Gombrich is equally impressed by the utility and longevity of many of these classifying systems: "For the ancient world and those that followed its teaching, the distinctions between hot and cold, moist and dry provided in their combinations the four basic categories sufficient to classify the humours of man, the seasons and the elements. It is quite a humbling excercise to study the success of these crude systems and to ponder its reasons." Gombrich, *Norm and Form,* 82.

25. Lethaby, discussing the cosmic symbolism that building once possessed, mentions how the ancient temple was governed by ideas derived from the science of the time; it was a heaven, an observatory, and an almanac. He thus renders concisely the multiple roles that architecture might have of representing an ahistorical ideal, of observing the historical present to compare it to this ideal, and finally of making some record of this continuing process. W. R. Lethaby, *Architecture, Mysticism and Myth* (1891), with an introduction and bibliography by Godfrey Rubens (New York: George Braziller, 1975), 5.

26. "Tradition is a matter of much wider significance. It cannot be inherited, and if you want it you must obtain it by great labour. It involves, in the first place, the historical sense, which we may call nearly indispensable to anyone who would continue to be a poet beyond his twenty-fifth year; and the historical sense involves a perception, not only of the pastness of the past, but of its presence; the historical sense compels a man to write not merely with his own generation in his bones, but with a feeling that the whole of literature of Europe from Homer and within it the whole of literature of his own country has a simultaneous existence and composes a simultaneous order. This historical sense, which is the sense of the timeless and of the temporal together, is what makes a writer more acutely conscious of his place in time, of his contemporaneity." Eliot, "Tradition and the Individual Talent," 14.

27. Collingwood, describing Greek thought, distinguishes thinking from opinion, which in the absence of reflection exists only in the most ephemeral state. "Opinion is the empirical semi-knowledge we have of matters of fact, which are always changing. It is our fleeting acquaintance with the fleeting actualities of the world; it thus only holds good for its own proper duration, for the here and now; and it is immediate, ungrounded in reasons, incapable of demonstration. True knowledge, on the contrary,

holds good not only here and now but everywhere and always, and it is based on demonstrative reasoning and thus capable of meeting and overthrowing error by the weapon of dialectical criticism." R. G. Collingwood, *The Idea of History* (London: Oxford University Press, 1946), 21.

28. "The central greatness of *Paradise Regained,* as a poem, is not the greatness of the rhetorical decorations that Milton added to his source, but the greatness of the theme itself, which Milton passes on to the reader from his source. This conception of the great poet's being entrusted with the great theme was elementary enough to Milton, but violates most of the low mimetic prejudices about creation that most of us are educated in." Frye, *Anatomy of Criticism,* 96.

When the young Bishop in Willa Cather's novel praises the onion soup he has been served he expresses thoughts close to those of Frye: "I am not deprecating your individual talent, Joseph . . . but, when one thinks of it, a soup like this is not the work of one man. It is the result of a constantly refined tradition. There are nearly a thousand years of history in this soup." Willa Cather, *Death Comes for the Archbishop* (1927; rpt. New York: Alfred A. Knopf, 1962), 39.

3 Action and Representation

1. Vico's account of the first human hypothesis regarding the structure and significance of the sky parallels that of Vitruvius, but Vico explains the origin of this hypothesis in a way that is only hinted at in Vitruvius. Vico's tale begins in the forest after his giants have experienced their first flash of lightning and bolt of thunder: "Thereupon a few giants, who must have been the most robust, and who were dispersed through the forests on the mountain heights where the strongest beasts have their dens, were frightened and astonished by the great effect whose cause they did not know, and raised their eyes and became aware of the sky. And because in such a case the nature of the human mind leads it to attribute its own nature to the effect, and because in that state their nature was that of men all robust bodily strength, who expressed their very violent passions by shouting and grumbling, they pictured the sky to themselves as a great animated body, which in that aspect they called Jove, the first god of the so-called greater gentes, who meant to tell them something by the hiss of his bolts and clap of his thunder." Giambattista Vico, *The New Science of Giambattista Vico,* trans. Thomas Goddard Bergin and Max Harold Fisch, rev. ed. (Ithaca: Cornell University Press, 1968), 117–118.

Although Vico has not yet proposed the clearing that was crucial to the Vitruvian myth, it could be argued that all of the requisite elements are already implicit in his story. Vico's sky, revealed by the lightning, operates as a parallel to the Vitruvian clearing, both of them openings within a dark and limitless forest that provide the necessary orientation for human action.

2. "Lastly, the conviction followed, that as nature neither had furnished nor could furnish any perfect and complete model for imitation, as regards art, so it remained for the genius of the artist itself to complete by a judicious combination, the qualities of the particular model." Antoine Chrysostome Quatremère de Quincy, *An Essay on the Nature, the End, and the Means of Imitation in the Fine Arts,* trans. J. C. Kent (London: Smith, Elder and Co., 1837), 223. The position that Quatremère takes here presumably derives from

Aristotle's similar claim that the purpose of the arts is "to supply the deficiencies of nature." *Politics* iv.(vii.)17.1337a 1–2, quoted in S. H. Butcher, *Aristotle's Theory of Poetry and Fine Art,* 4th ed. (New York: Dover, 1951), 119 n. 3. All further quotations from Aristotle are from the Butcher translation. Butcher writes that "the state is indeed a natural institution, but needs the political art to organize it and to realize nature's full idea." Ibid., 119.

Austin writes: "Homeric thought, seeing the whole natural world unified into a single complex of space and time, then attempts to have everything conform to that order. . . . Man, as a part of nature, is already of that order, but it is also his task to contribute to the maintenance of that order by imitation." Norman Austin, *Archery at the Dark of the Moon: Poetic Problems in Homer's "Odyssey"* (Berkeley: University of California Press, 1975), 104.

3. Thus Collingwood describes Vico's contention regarding the limits of human knowledge: understanding something, as opposed to merely perceiving it, can only occur when the knower himself could have made it. R. G. Collingwood, *The Idea of History* (London: Oxford University Press, 1946), 64.

Summerson, discussing the classical orders, observes that the architect so identifies with the orders that he almost believes himself to have designed them. He quotes Lutyens: "That time-worn Doric order—a lovely thing—I have the cheek to adopt. You can't copy it. To be right you have to take it and design it . . . if you tackle it in this way, the order belongs to you." John Summerson, *The Classical Language of Architecture* (Cambridge: MIT Press, 1963), 19.

4. Raymond Williams's essay on the word *represent* is most helpful for understanding the rich and varied potential of the word. Williams, *Keywords: A Vocabulary of Culture and Society* (New York: Oxford University Press, 1983), 266.

5. In this regard, representation operates similarly to other forms of symbolic thinking such as myth. "Myth, art, language and science appear as symbols; not in the sense of mere figures which refer to some given reality by means of suggestion and allegorical renderings, but in the sense of forces each of which produces and posits a world of its own. . . . Thus the special symbolic forms are not imitations, but organs of reality, since it is solely by their agency that anything real becomes an object for intellectual apprehension, and as such is made visible to us." Ernst Cassirer, *Language and Myth,* trans. Susanne Langer (1946; rpt. New York: Dover, 1953), 8.

"Myth lives by the intensity with which it seizes and takes possession of consciousness in a specific moment. Myth lacks any means of extending the moment beyond itself." Cassirer, *The Philosophy of Symbolic Forms,* trans. Ralph Manheim, 4 vols. (New Haven: Yale University Press, 1955), 2:35.

A necessary consequence of this condition is the recognition that myth does not merely stand for the object but has the same actuality, so that it replaces the thing's immediate presence much the way rites, in preceding myths, should not be viewed as allegorical but as absolutely real. For further elaboration see Cassirer, "The Mythical Consciousness of the Object," in ibid.

6. Scott dismisses the romantic architecture of his era, which took on the surface attributes of spatially and temporally remote architectural styles in the belief that the

corresponding social ethic might accompany them. Instead, he sees architecture as becoming significant due to our direct sensuous response to its form and substance. Geoffrey Scott, "The Romantic Fallacy," in *The Architecture of Humanism*, 2d ed. (Garden City, N.Y.: Doubleday, 1924).

7. Giving the example of the irregular landscape garden, Quatremère writes that it offers no pleasure in terms of imitation since it seeks to erase any artifice necessary for imitation; nor is it nature itself, since it is in fact artifice disguised. Quatremère, *Essay*, 171.

8. Eco describes how a sign both promotes an action and signifies something about that particular action, giving the example of the spoon whose use fulfills a particular function while at the same time communicating a conformity with specific societal expectations about eating. Umberto Eco, "Function and Sign: Semiotics of Architecture," in *Structures Implicit and Explicit*, VIA 2 (Philadelphia: Graduate School of Fine Arts, University of Pennsylvania, 1973), 131.

9. Cassirer wishes to avoid the reductive simplification toward which the universal ultimately leads, and yet not get lost in the particularity of individual phenomena such that no return to the universal is possible. "An escape from this methodological dilemma is possible only if we can discover a factor which recurs in each basic cultural form but in no two of them takes exactly the same shape. Then . . . we might assert the ideal relation between the individual provinces—between the basic functions of language and cognition, of art and religion—without losing the incomparable particularity of any one of them. . . . It is the fundamental principle of cognition that the universal can be perceived only in the particular, while the particular can be thought only in reference to the universal." Cassirer, *Philosophy of Symbolic Forms*, 2:84–86.

10. Analyzing Aristotle's conception of tragedy, Butcher explains: "The dramatic action must be so significant, and its meaning capable of such extension, that through it we can discern the higher laws which rule the world. The private life of an individual, tragic as it may be in its inner quality, has never been made the subject of the highest tragedy. . . . The tragic Katharsis requires . . . that the deeds and fortunes of the actors shall attach themselves to larger issues, and the spectator himself be lifted above the special case and brought face to face with universal law and the divine plan of the world." Butcher, *Aristotle*, 270–271. In distinguishing between poetry and history, Aristotle observes: "It is not the function of the poet to relate what has happened, but what may happen, what is possible according to the law of probability or necessity" (*Poetics* ix), and: "For poetry tends to express the universal, history the particular" (*Poetics* ix.3). Butcher further comments on this: "The capacity of poetry is so far limited that it expresses the universal not as it is in itself, but as seen though the medium of sensuous imagery," and: "The aim of poetry is to represent the universal through the particular, to give a concrete and living embodiment of a universal truth." Ibid., 191–192. This is further qualified: "Greek tragedies, though 'founded on fact' . . . transmute that fact into imaginative truth." Ibid., 170.

Similarly, André Gide is reported to have described history as fiction that has come true, while fiction is history that has not yet taken place.

11. In the *New Science*, Vico makes a case for the importance of abstraction. Of the prehuman condition, he writes that "their minds were so limited to particulars that they regarded every change in facial expression as a new face" (700), and that their minds "took things one at a time, being in this respect little better than the minds of beasts, for which each new sensation cancels the last one (which is the cause of their being unable to compare and reason discursively)" (703).

Vico, like Vitruvius, places this prehuman condition within the forest, a dark, limitless field without orientation, and therefore without place, where the particular reigns. It will require the clearing, with all of its implicit orientational and structural apparatus, to establish the conditions necessary for synthetic reasoning and bring the myriad particular sensations of the forest into a coherent and comprehensive world.

12. This parallels Frye's account of the production of meaning in literary works. "Works of literature also move in time like music and spread out in images like painting. The word narrative or *mythos* conveys the sense of movement caught by the ear, and the word meaning or *dianoia* conveys, or at least preserves, the sense of simultaneity caught by the eye. We listen to the poem as it moves from beginning to end, but as soon as the whole of it is in our minds at once we 'see' what it means. More exactly this response is not simply to the whole of it, but to a whole in it: we have a vision of meaning . . . whenever any simultaneous apprehension is possible." Northrop Frye, *Anatomy of Criticisms: Four Essays* (Princeton: Princeton University Press, 1957), 77–78.

What the reader "sees" when apprehending "a whole in it" is a spatial structure formed as a hypothesis in response to the text. This image takes in all the diverse pieces of the work and sets them into a comprehensible unity, larger than the work itself because it now includes the reader. Thus meaning is neither static nor singular as something only embedded in the text, but rather comes into existence through a collaboration between text and imagination. The complex exchange between the temporal and spatial dimensions that Frye describes is crucial to this process and is what allows or even commands the reader's engagement.

13. "When we attribute a certain size, position, and distance to things in space, we are not thereby expressing a simple datum of sensation but are situating the sensory data in a relationship and system, which proves ultimately to be nothing other than a relationship of pure judgement." Cassirer, *Philosophy of Symbolic Forms*, 2:30.

14. For the mythic importance of the tree, see Sir James George Frazer, "The Worship of Trees," in *The Golden Bough*, abr. ed. (New York: Macmillan, 1963), chap. 9.

15. Vitruvius, *The Ten Books on Architecture*, trans. Morris Hicky Morgan (Cambridge: Harvard University Press, 1914), 103–106.

16. Gombrich points out that the terminology of art history is generally based on principles of exclusion. Certain taboos are erected to distinguish one style from that which preceded it. This results in the elevation of difference over qualities that might be shared. This observation applies also to artistic creation operating within a historicist ideology where ideas become so attached to a particular style that their independence is severely compromised and their use at any other time is questionable. E. H. Gombrich, *Norm and Form* (London: Phaidon, 1966), 89.

17. For Aristotle, imitation is an inherent part of human nature. "First, the instinct of imitation is implanted in man from childhood, one difference between him and other animals being that he is the most imitative of living creatures, and through imitation learns his earliest lessons; and no less universal is the pleasure felt in things imitated" (*Poetics* iv.2). Aristotle seems to be suggesting an inherent value that accrues to the mental exercise of comparing the poetic imitation to its object and discovering the means by which the two are related.

Compare the comments of Le Corbusier and Ozenfant: "One of the highest delights of the human mind is to perceive the order of nature and to measure its own participation in the scheme of things; the work of art seems to us to be a labor of putting into order, a masterpiece of human order." Le Corbusier and Amédée Ozenfant, "Purism," in Robert L. Herbert, ed., *Modern Artists on Art* (Englewood Cliffs, N.J.: Prentice-Hall, 1964).

18. "Leonardo achieved his greatest triumph of lifelike expression by blurring precisely the features in which expression resides, thus compelling us to complete the act of creation." E. H. Gombrich, "Meditations on a Hobby Horse," in Morris Philipson, eds., *Aesthetics Today* (Cleveland: World Publishing, 1961), 125. Recall also Gombrich's discussion of the hobby horse, as representation, referred to in chapter 1, note 12, above.

19. Aristotle's writing on imitation in the *Poetics* is a necessary starting point for the discussion of abstraction as a means of representing significant ideas of our world. His use of abstraction as a critical tool relating the particular to the universal is especially useful for understanding most subsequent writing on typology. I would, however, side with those who are skeptical about Aristotle's belief that these systems of classification are inherent in the natural world.

20. "An increase in naturalism means a decrease in order. It is clear, I think, that most artistic value rests among other things on the exact reconciliation of these conflicting demands. Primitive art, on the whole, is an art of rigid symmetries sacrificing plausibility to a wonderful sense of pattern, while the art of the impressionists went so far in its search for visual truth as to appear almost to discard the principle of order altogether." Gombrich, *Norm and Form*, 94.

21. Frye describes the paradox that the most recondite writers whose work requires patient study are explicitly mythopoeic: "Learned mythopoeia . . . may become bewilderingly complex; but the complexities are designed to reveal and not to disguise the myth." Frye sees Shakespeare's late plays as tending more toward the archaic and being more suggestive of myth and ritual, yet these plays come closest to understanding what our whole literary experience is about. Frye, *Anatomy of Criticism*, 117.

22. I am indebted to the research of Scholes and Kellogg for my understanding of the workings of oral narration. See Robert Scholes and Robert Kellogg, "The Oral Heritage of Written Narrative," in *The Nature of Narrative* (London: Oxford University Press, 1966).

23. Hannah Arendt offers some of the most profound modern criticism of the meaning of the public realm; her thoughts on speech and action are crucial to my thesis. "Human

plurality, the basic condition of both action and speech, has the twofold character of equality and distinction. If men were not equal, they could neither understand each other and those who came before them nor plan for the future and foresee the needs of those who will come after them. If men were not distinct, each human being distinguished from any other who is, was, or will ever be, they would need neither speech nor action to make themselves understood. Signs and sounds to communicate immediate, identical needs and wants would be enough. . . . Speech and action reveal this distinctness. Through them, men distinguish themselves instead of being merely distinct; they are the modes in which human beings appear to each other, not indeed as physical objects, but *qua* men. . . . A life without speech and without action . . . is literally dead to the world; it has ceased to be a human life because it is no longer lived among men. . . . To act . . . means to take an initiative, to begin . . . to set something into motion. . . . In acting and speaking, men show who they are. . . . This revelatory quality of speech and action comes to the fore where people are with others . . . in sheer human togetherness." Hannah Arendt, *The Human Condition* (Chicago: University of Chicago Press, 1958), 175–180.

Eliot similarly observes about the personality of the artist and the content of the art: "What happens is a continual surrender of himself as he is at the moment to something which is more valuable. The progress of an artist is a continual self-sacrifice, a continual extinction of personality." T. S. Eliot, "Tradition and the Individual Talent," in *Selected Essays, 1917–1932* (London: Faber and Faber, 1961), 17. "Poetry is not a turning loose of emotion, but an escape from emotion; it is not the expression of personality, but an escape from personality. But, of course, only those who have personality and emotions know what it means to want to escape from these things." Ibid., 21.

Arendt explains the Greek polis as a place constituted in response to this condition of the human. "The polis was supposed to multiply the occasions to win 'immortal fame,' that is, to multiply the chances for everybody to distinguish himself, to show in deed and word who he was in his unique distinctness. . . . The second function of the polis . . . was to offer a remedy for the futility of action and speech; for the chances that a deed deserving fame would not be forgotten, that it actually would become 'immortal,' were not very good. Homer was not only a shining example of the poet's political function, and therefore the 'educator of all Hellas'; the very fact that so great an enterprise as the Trojan War could have been forgotten without a poet to immortalize it several hundred years later offered only too good an example of what could happen to human greatness if it had nothing but poets to rely on for its permanence. . . . The polis—if we trust the famous words of Pericles in the Funeral Oration—gives a guaranty that those who forced every sea and land to become the scene of their daring will not remain without witness and will need neither Homer nor anyone else who knows how to turn words to praise them; without assistance from others, those who acted will be able to establish together the everlasting remembrance of their good and bad deeds, to inspire admiration in the present and in future ages. In other words, men's life together in the form of the polis seemed to assure that the most futile of human activities, action and speech, and the least tangible and most ephemeral of man-made 'products,' the deeds and stories which are their outcome, would become imperishable. The organization of the polis, physically secured by the wall around the city and physiognomically guaranteed by its laws—lest the succeeding generations change its identity beyond recognition—is a kind of organized remembrance. It assures the mortal actor that his passing existence and fleeting greatness will never lack the reality that comes from being seen, being heard, and, generally, appearing before an audience of fellow men, who outside the polis could attend only the short duration of the performance and therefore needed Homer and 'others of his craft' in order to be presented to those who were not there." Arendt, *Human Condition*, 197–198.

Eliade comments that one of the unexpected qualities of the image or symbol is its ability to bring people together more effectively and more genuinely than any analytical language. It is this quality that makes the polis capable of the role attributed to it by Arendt. See Mircea Eliade, *Images and Symbols: Studies in Religious Symbolism*, trans. Philip Mairet (New York: Sheed and Ward, 1969), 17.

24. Among other problems, the Hegelian legacy has left us with less appreciation for the value of the historical event itself. Since history in the post-Hegelian view, is progressing toward an unknown goal only able to be disclosed in the future, its particular manifestation at any moment along the way can only be in an imperfectly realized state of becoming and consequently inadequate as an exemplar for our actions. If history is to have a role in continuing to define the view we have of ourselves and our world, it will need to operate in a more paradigmatic manner and will need to look to other sources for its theory. Eliade sees "mythical history" as directly engaged in making hypotheses about the structure of the world and our place within this by replicating its conclusions through ritual. This replication is profoundly at odds with Hegel: "Modern man though regarding himself as the result of Universal History does not feel obliged to know the whole of it, the man of the archaic societies is not only obliged to remember mythical history but also to *re-enact* a large part of it periodically." Mircea Eliade, *Myth and Reality*, trans. Willard R. Trask (New York: Harper and Row, 1963), 13.

Collingwood's inquiry into the purpose of history forces him to look outside its linear causality in order to find a constancy that could claim authority as principle. He concludes, similarly to Eliade, that "knowing yourself means knowing what you can do; and since nobody knows what he can do until he tries, the only clue to what man can do is what man has done. The value of history, then, is that it teaches us what man has done and thus what man is." Collingwood, *Idea of History*, 10.

Austin's analysis of the *Odyssey* also calls attention to its paradigmatic value: "The past is cogent because it is human experience fixed and structured. Homeric heroes find in paradigm a permanent pattern which can give shape to their ephemeral lives and actions." Austin, *Archery*, 125.

Frye explicitly rejects claims about progress in the arts. Rather than improving, the purpose of the arts is to produce models: "What does improve in the arts is the comprehension of them, and the refining of society which results from it. . . . The profoundest experiences possible to obtain in the arts are available in the art already produced." Frye, *Anatomy of Criticism*, 344.

Eliot, while also dismissing the idea of improvement, does value change, not, however, for itself, but for revealing additional hypotheses all of which claim legitimacy to varying degrees: "[The poet] must be aware of the obvious fact that art never improves, but that the material of art is never quite the same. He must be aware that the mind of Europe—the mind of his own country—a mind which he learns in time to be much more important than his own private mind—is a mind which changes, and that this change is a development which abandons nothing en route, which does not superannuate either Shakespeare, or Homer, or the rock drawings of the Magdalenian draughtsmen." Eliot, "Tradition and the Individual Talent," 16.

See also Robert Jan Van Pelt, "Heraclitean Heritance," in Robert Jan Van Pelt and Carroll William Westfall, *Architectural Principles in the Age of Historicism* (New Haven: Yale University Press, 1991).

25. This is a quality essential to the understanding of myth and one also shared by the paradigm, since at the most fundamental level the task of the paradigm is the proposing of relationships. "Mythical thought, in fact, expects at every instant metamorphosis at the corporal level but stability at the deeper level of relationship." Austin, *Archery,* 128

26. This loose fit is a crucial property in allowing the plan to operate symbolically. Langer refers to this quality in symbols as "indifference" and states that "the more barren and indifferent the symbol, the greater is its semantic power." Susanne K. Langer, *Philosophy in a New Key* (New York: Mentor Books, 1948), 61.

27. In his incisive analysis of the relationship between the architectural plan and patterns of domestic existence, Robin Evans illustrates how the plan works literally to promote relationships by the structure and situation of windows, doors, stairs, etc., while at the same time communicating the import of these relationships as a sign, independent of the need to physically pass through the building. Robin Evans, "Figures, Doors and Passages," *Architectural Design* 48 (1978), 267–278.

This meaning of the sign is based on Langer's description: "[Signs] serve . . . to let us develop a characteristic attitude toward objects in absentia, which is called 'thinking of' or 'referring to' what is not here. 'Signs' used in this capacity are not symptoms of things but symbols." Langer, *Philosophy in a New Key,* 24.

28. Geoffrey Scott points out the important but often neglected distinction between content and form and the meaning that each of these might aspire to. He gives the example of the strange, fantastic, and unexpected being represented by Coleridge through a medium (poetry) that was simple, familiar, and fixed. He extends this to architecture to show how the "magical Casements" are a powerful image in Keats's poetry because they are imagined, whereas a literal realization in building would result in disappointment since they would open "not on the 'foam of perilous seas,' but, most often, upon a landscape-garden less faery than forlorn." In other words, the meaning that poetry is able to convey through the conventions of language should not be confused with the meaning that the structure of architecture can produce as it is immediately experienced. Scott, *Architecture of Humanism,* 65.

29. For an excellent account of the historical basis of architecture's response to the supposed superiority of literary meaning due to the modern production of printed books, see Neil Levine, "The Romantic Idea of Architectural Legibility: Henri Labrouste and the Neo-Grec," in *The Architecture of the Ecole des Beaux-Arts,* ed. Arthur Drexler (New York: Museum of Modern Art, 1977); also Neil Levine, "The Book and the Building: Hugo's Theory of Architecture and Labrouste's Bibliothèque Ste.-Geneviève," in Robin Middleton, ed., *The Beaux-Arts and Nineteenth-Century French Architecture* (Cambridge: MIT Press, 1982).

For a slightly different account, see Joseph Rykwert, "The Purpose of Ceremonies: Categories of Social Action in the City and Archdeacon Frollo's Observations," *Lotus International* 17, no. 4 (1977), 57–61.

30. Frye makes a similar point: "A poem's meaning is literally its pattern or integrity as a verbal structure. Its words cannot be separated and attached to sign-values: all possible sign-values of a word are absorbed into a complexity of verbal relationships." Frye, *Anatomy of Criticism,* 78.

4 The Structure of Paradigms

1. "Thus all things are known by comparison. . . . Since man is the thing best known to man, perhaps Protagoras, by saying that man is the mode and measure of all things, meant that all the accidents of things are known through comparison to the accidents of man." Leon Battista Alberti, *On Painting,* trans. with introduction and notes by John R. Spencer (New Haven: Yale University Press, 1966), 55.

As modern science has increasingly treated its descriptions of both space and time as abstractions removed from our actions within them, it has disengaged the mythical unity of space and time. Language, however, is more resistant to these impulses, and often retains clues that allow us to trace the changing contexts within which it has developed. This is evident in Pollitt's observations on how the physical movements of dance (which are in essence spatial locations) are linked to the temporal structure of poetry and music. "ρύθμοι [*rhythmoi*] were originally the positions that the human body was made to assume in the course of a dance, in other words the patterns or schemata that the body made. In the course of a dance certain obvious patterns or positions, like the raising or lowering of a foot, were naturally repeated, thus marking intervals in the dance. Since music and singing were synchronized with dancing, the recurrent positions taken by the dancer in the course of his movements also marked distinct intervals. . . . This explains why the basic component of music and poetry was called a πους, 'foot.'" J. J. Pollitt, *The Ancient View of Greek Art* (New Haven: Yale University Press, 1974), 138–139, quoted in W. J. T. Mitchell, "Spatial Form in Literature," in W. J. T. Mitchell, ed., *The Language of Images* (Chicago: University of Chicago Press, 1980), 280.

"But clearly the contrast between heat and cold makes sense only in relation to a norm, mostly the hidden norm of our own body temperature. Science, of course, tries to eliminate this norm and prefers to plot temperature along a scale." E. H. Gombrich, *Norm and Form* (London: Phaidon, 1966), 93.

2. "Religious man's desire to live in the sacred is in fact equivalent to his desire to take up his abode in objective reality, not to let himself be paralysed by the never-ceasing relativity of purely subjective experience. . . . Religious man feels the need always to exist in a total and organized world, in a cosmos." Mircea Eliade, *The Sacred and the Profane: The Nature of Religion,* trans. Willard R. Trask (New York: Harcourt, Brace and World, 1959), 28, 44.

3. Lewis Thomas observes that it is our almost unlimited capacity for worry that distinguishes the human from other forms of life. See Lewis Thomas, "On Transcendental Metaworry (TMW)," in *The Medusa and the Snail* (New York: Bantam Press, 1979).

4. "The conquest of the superfluous gives us a greater spiritual excitement than the conquest of the necessary. Man is a creation of desire, not a creation of necessity." Gaston Bachelard, *The Psychoanalysis of Fire,* trans. Alan Ross (Boston: Beacon Press, 1964), 16.

5. "We comfort ourselves by reliving memories of protection. Something closed must retain our memories . . . memories of the outside world will never have the same tonality as those of the home." Gaston Bachelard, *The Poetics of Space*, trans. Maria Jolas (Boston: Beacon Press, 1964), 6. The home that Bachelard mentions, however, must be understood in a fundamentally more profound context: "For our house is our corner of the world . . . it is our first universe, a real cosmos in every sense of the word." Ibid., 4.

6. This is also an important quality of mythical thinking: "Mythical thought always progresses from the awareness of oppositions towards their resolution." Claude Lévi-Strauss, *Structural Anthropology*, trans. Claire Jacobson and Brooke Grundfest Schoepf (New York: Basic Books, 1963), 224.

7. "What better proof is there that the contemplation of fire brings us back to the very origins of philosophic thought? If fire, which after all, is quite an exceptional and rare phenomenon, was taken to be a constituent element of the Universe, is it not because it is an element of human thought, the prime element of reverie?" Bachelard, *Psychoanalysis of Fire*, 18.

Fustel de Coulanges's description of the hearth in ancient Greece and Rome reveals its complex engagement in almost all domestic rituals, so that it became the determining factor of domesticity itself. Every house contained an altar on which were always maintained a small quantity of ashes and a few lighted coals. The rules and the rites that each house observed regarding this hearth/altar show that it was a significant part of life. The fire ceased to glow upon the altar only when the entire family had perished. This is recorded in synonymous expressions for the extinguished hearth and the extinguished family. Although otherwise kept burning, the fire was ritually put out one day a year and immediately rekindled to ensure its purity. The only means allowable to restart the fire were to focus the solar rays or rub together rapidly two pieces of wood of a particular sort. Flint or steel were prohibited. A man never left his dwelling before addressing a prayer to the fire and upon return would invoke the fire even before seeing his wife or embracing his children. "Thus the hearth-fire is a sort of a moral being; it shines, and warms, and cooks the sacred food; but at the same time it thinks, and has a conscience; it knows men's duties, and sees that they are fulfilled. One might call it human, for it has the double nature of man; physically it blazes up, it moves, it lives, it procures abundance, it prepares the repast, it nourishes the body; morally, it has sentiments and affections, it gives man purity, it enjoins the beautiful and the good, it nourishes the soul. . . . Later, when they made the great Vesta of this myth of the sacred fire, Vesta was the virgin goddess. She represented in the world neither fecundity nor power; she was order, but not rigorous, abstract, mathematical order . . . she was moral order. They imagined her as a sort of universal soul, which regulated the different movements of worlds, as the human soul keeps order in the human system." Numa Fustel de Coulanges, *The Ancient City* (Garden City, N.Y.: Doubleday, 1956), 22–33.

Compare this with Bachelard's description: "It shines in Paradise. It burns in Hell. It is gentleness and torture. It is cookery and it is apocalypse. It is pleasure for the good child sitting prudently by the hearth; yet it punishes any disobedience when the child wishes to play too close to its flames. It is well being and it is respect. It is a tutelary and a terrible divinity, both good and bad. It can be contradictory itself; thus it is one of the principles of universal explanation." Bachelard, *Psychoanalysis of Fire*, 7.

Fustel de Coulanges also shows how the hearth, whose etymology indicates its appropriateness to represent a life firmly attached to a specific place, is metaphorically and physically grounded in the earth. When the hearth is established the god is installed in that particular place for as long as the family shall endure. It was from this religious belief that the political concept of private property was to develop so as to protect the hearth and thus the sanctity of the home. Fustel de Coulanges, *Ancient City,* 60.

8. For an interpretation of myths and rituals that relate to the idea of center, see Eliade, "The Center of the World," in *Sacred and Profane.* For a discussion of properties of the center see Mircea Eliade, "Symbolism of the Center," in *Images and Symbols: Studies in Religious Symbolism,* trans. Philip Mairet (New York: Sheed and Ward, 1969).

9. "For religious man, space is not homogeneous; he experiences interruptions, breaks in it; some parts of space are qualitatively different from others. . . . This spatial nonhomogeneity finds expression in the experience of an opposition between space that is sacred—the only real and real-ly existing space—and all other space, the formless expanse surrounding it. . . . For it is the break effected in space that allows the world to be constituted, because it reveals the fixed point, the central axis for all future orientation. . . . Nothing can begin, nothing can be done, without a previous orientation—and any orientation implies acquiring a fixed point. It is for this reason that religious man has always sought to fix his abode at 'the center of the world.'" Eliade, *Sacred and Profane,* 20–22.

10. This quality of the boundary as a "magical" defense is developed in Eliade, *Images and Symbols,* 39.

11. It is possible to argue that it is the unfolding of this neutral Cartesian spatial ordering, with its emptiness, that has caused us to look away from our constructed world, tied as it is to the Cartesian model. We now have to turn to the world of nature in a search for places of authentic character. While recognizing that nature is no substitute for places closer to our own distinct purposes, we also realize the need to preserve this rapidly dwindling resource as a catalyst for a more meaningful reconstitution of our own world.

12. An excellent analysis of the significance of space and its relationship to time in Homeric poetry is found in Norman Austin, *Archery at the Dark of the Moon: Poetic Problems in Homer's "Odyssey"* (Berkeley: University of California Press, 1975), 101–102. Austin notes that it is because space has quality that we are entitled to find significance in the gestures of the Homeric gods. Their actions are played out in a space within whose coordinates orientation becomes an expression of psychological condition understood by both actor and reader. "Space [in the *Odyssey*] is not a linear continuum divisible into miles and furlongs, or stadia and parasangs, but a nexus of visual activities. Distance is measured by its relation to human experience. It is an unladen ship cutting through the sea daylong under full sail, a man's shout across the water, a day's ploughing . . . the cast of a herdsman's staff." Ibid., 89.

13. Bergson gives an account of how we naturally perceive the two sides of our body (the left and right) as having different qualities. See Henri Bergson, *Time and Free Will,* trans. F. L. Pogson (1910; rpt. London: Allen and Unwin, 1950), 97.

14. Thus far, the ground has been presented in somewhat abstract terms. It is important to acknowledge meanings within the soil itself and the consequent quality of undergroundness that have had a strong effect on human consciousness. Fustel de Coulanges describes ancient Greek religion as being a religion of the dead, with ancestors as the object of worship well before there was an idea of a Zeus. The soul of the dead did not depart for a foreign world, rather it continued to live underground in close proximity to the living and required regular attention. This gave to the soil a meaning considerably more profound and engaged than the present valuation of the earth as a mere commodity. In fact, a man could not quit his dwelling place without taking with him his soil, or in other words his ancestors. Fustel de Coulanges, *Ancient City*, 136.

The hearth was also engaged in this veneration of the ancestors, with its sacred fire representing their constant presence. Hearth and soil are thus intertwined in a complex and intense relationship. While the hearth's vertical extension is its most obvious visible attribute, we also see that, with its foundations firmly grounded in the earth, it implies extension down into the ground, creating an axial connection among underground, ground, and sky. Ibid., 61.

Although Bachelard's research into the phenomenology of the house concentrates on the poetic rather than the historic, the particular loading of the underground that he describes would seem either to derive from the condition that Fustel shows or else to be evidence of an even more primal understanding. For instance: "The cellar dreamer knows that the walls of the cellar are buried walls, that they are walls with a single casing, walls that have the entire earth behind them." Bachelard, "The House, from Cellar to Garret: The Significance of the Hut," in *Poetics of Space*, 20.

A quality shared by these interpretations is the actual or implied absence of form in the underground. Without form, the underground lacks the orientational structure fundamental to making a place. Eliade gives the example of the primordial snake, a creature without form, and shows how it becomes the symbol of darkness, night, and death, or in other words of the amorphous and virtual of everything that has not yet acquired a form. Eliade, *Sacred and Profane*, 48.

15. Eliade notes that all forms of cosmos have an opening above enabling passage from one mode of being to another. "Man passes from pre-life to life and finally to death. . . . Human existence attains completion through a series of 'passage' rites or successive initiations." Eliade, *Sacred and Profane*, 180–181.

16. The strength of the symbolic structure of the center seems incongruous with the simplicity of its geometrical construction. When reduced to this sign, its dismissal in contemporary thought seems valid enough. Analytical description always fails the symbol, making it necessary to rely on the very mechanisms of imitation, representation, and symbolic thinking that I have described in the last two chapters. Borges's confrontation with the center, and his discussion of the inadequacies of discursive writing to represent this confrontation, give a hint of the immense potential of the most fundamental of all paradigmatic structures.

> "It's in the dining-room cellar," he explained, his diction grown hasty from anxiety. . . . The cellar stair is steep, and my aunt and uncle had forbidden me to go down it. But someone said that there was a world in the cellar. They were referring,

I found out later, to a trunk, but I understood there was a world there. I descended secretly, went rolling down the forbidden stair, fell off. When I opened my eyes I saw the Aleph. "Yes, the Place where, without any possible confusion, all the places in the world are found, seen from every angle."

When the protagonist enters the cellar, this is what he finds:

I arrive, now, at the ineffable centre of my story. And here begins my despair as a writer. All language is an alphabet of symbols whose use presupposes a past shared by all the other interlocutors. How, then, transmit to others the infinite Aleph, which my fearful mind scarcely encompasses? The mystics, in similar situations, are lavish with emblems: to signify the divinity, a Persian speaks of a bird that in some way is all birds; Alanus de Insulis speaks of a sphere whose centre is everywhere and whose circumference is nowhere; Ezekiel, of an angel with four faces who looks simultaneously to the Orient and the Occident to the North and the South. (Not vainly do I recall these inconceivable analogies; they bear some relation to the Aleph.) Perhaps the gods would not be against my finding an equivalent image, but then this report would be contaminated with literature, with falsehood. For the rest, the central problem is unsolvable: the enumeration, even if only partial, of an infinite complex. In that gigantic instant I saw millions of delights and atrocious acts; none astonished me more than the fact that all of them together occupied the same point, without superposition and without transparency. What my eyes saw was simultaneous: what I shall transcribe is successive, because language is successive. Nevertheless, I shall cull something of it all.

In the lower part of the step, towards the right, I saw a small iridescent sphere, of almost intolerable brilliance. At first I thought it rotary; then I understood that this movement was an illusion produced by the vertiginous sights it enclosed. The Aleph's diameter must have been about two or three centimeters, but Cosmic Space was in it, without diminution of size. Each object (the mirror's glass, for instance) was infinite objects, for I clearly saw it from all points in the universe. I saw the heavy-laden sea; I saw the dawn and the dusk; I saw the multitudes of America; I saw a silver-plated cobweb at the centre of a black pyramid; I saw a tattered labyrinth (it was London); I saw interminable eyes nearby looking at me as if in a mirror; I saw all the mirrors in the planet and none reflected me; in an inner patio in the Calle Soler I saw the same paving tile I had seen thirty years before in the entrance way to a house in the town of Fray Bentos; I saw clusters of grapes, snow, tobacco, veins of metal, steam; I saw convex equatorial deserts and every grain of sand in them; I saw a woman at Inverness whom I shall not forget: I saw her violent switch of hair, her proud body, the cancer in her breast; I saw a circle of dry land in a sidewalk where formerly there had been a tree; I saw a villa in Adrogué; I saw a copy of the first English version of Pliny, by Philemon Holland, and saw simultaneously every letter on every page (as a boy I used to marvel that the letters in a closed book did not get mixed up and lost in the course of a night); I saw night and day contemporaneously; I saw a sunset in Querétaro which seemed to reflect the colour of a rose in Bengal; I saw my bedroom with nobody in it; I saw in a study in Alkmaar a terraqueous globe between two mirrors which multiplied it without end; I saw horses with swirling manes on a beach by the Caspian Sea at dawn; I saw the delicate bone structure of a hand; I saw the survivors of a battle sending out postcards; I saw a deck of Spanish playing cards in a shop window in Mirzapur; I saw the oblique shadows of some ferns on the floor of a hothouse; I saw tigers, emboli, bison, ground swells, and armies; I saw all the ants on earth; I saw a Persian astrolabe; in a desk drawer I saw (the writing made me tremble) obscene, incredible, precise letters, which Beatriz had written Carlos Argentino; I saw an adored monument in La Chacarita cemetery; I saw the atrocious relic of what deliciously had been Beatriz Viterbo; I saw the circulation of my obscure blood; I saw the gearing of love and the modifications of death; I saw the Aleph from all points; I saw the earth in the Aleph and in the earth the Aleph once more and the earth in the Aleph; I saw my face and my viscera; I saw your face and felt vertigo and cried because my eyes had seen that conjectural and secret object whose name men usurp but which no man has gazed on: the inconceivable universe. I felt infinite veneration, infinite compassion."

Jorge Luis Borges, "The Aleph," in *A Personal Anthology* (London: Pan Books, 1972), 119–122.

17. Bachelard outlines two principal connecting themes that give order to the house. The first is its verticality and the second is its concentration, which "appeals to our consciousness of centrality." Verticality is ensured by the polarity of attic and cellar, which to Bachelard present the coupled opposing conditions of rationality and irrationality. The attic "tells its raison d'etre right away . . . up near the roof all our thoughts are clear . . . here we participate in the carpenter's solid geometry. . . . [The cellar] is first and foremost the dark entity of the house, the one that partakes of subterranean forces. . . . In the attic, the day's experiences can always efface the fears of night. In the cellar, darkness prevails both day and night, and even when we are carrying a lighted candle, we see shadows dancing on the dark walls." Bachelard, *Poetics of Space*, 17–19.
 Eliade also shows how at the center the three cosmic levels of earth, heaven, and underworld have been put into communication. Eliade, *Sacred and Profane*, 36.
 As an example of this connection, Fustel de Coulanges mentions the advice to locate the ancient Greek family tomb as near as possible to the door of the house in order that those entering and leaving might "meet" and presumably consult with their ancestors. Fustel de Coulanges, *Ancient City*, 36.

18. For a discussion of rites of ascension and their relationship to center through the means of the stair, see Eliade, *Images and Symbols*, 50.

19. There is a significant asymmetry between inside and outside as established by the boundary. "To make inside concrete and outside vast is the first task . . . of an anthropology of the imagination . . . inside and outside as experienced by the imagination, can no longer be taken in their simple reciprocity." Bachelard, *Poetics of Space*, 215–216. "The inward and the outward do not stand side by side, each as a separate province; each, rather, is reflected in the other, and only in this reciprocal reflection does each disclose its own meaning." Ernst Cassirer, *The Philosophy of Symbolic Forms*, trans. Ralph Manheim, 4 vols. (New Haven: Yale University Press, 1955), 2:99.

20. Martienssen observes that although a formally constructed horizontal surface of finite dimensions provides the material basis for an architectural arrangement, it still requires the wall to "reflect" the perception of the spectator and hold it within the

arrangement. His use of the term "reflect" is notable in that it demands a reciprocity between the wall and the spectator and further suggests that the consequent sense of enclosure is actually initiated by the spectator. Rex Distin Martienssen, *The Idea of Space in Greek Architecture*, 2d ed. (Johannesburg: Witwatersrand University Press, 1964), 6.

21. "One of the outstanding characteristics of traditional societies is the opposition that they assume between their inhabited territory and the unknown and indeterminate space that surrounds it. The former is the world (more precisely, our world), the cosmos; everything outside is no longer a cosmos but a sort of 'other world', a foreign, chaotic space, peopled by ghosts, demons, 'foreigners'." Eliade, *Sacred and Profane*, 29.

22. Douglas's research on the concepts of pollution and taboo shows how dirt is a concept defined by a culture's characteristic ideas of order. "Dirt is essentially disorder. There is no such thing as absolute dirt. . . . In chasing dirt . . . we are not governed by anxiety to escape disease, but are positively re-ordering our environment, making it conform to an idea." Mary Douglas, *Purity and Danger* (London: Ark, 1984), 2.

Frye makes the point that boundaries also create oppositions that were not necessarily intended in the original thinking. "There is however a moral dialectic in desire. The conception of a garden develops the conception 'weed', and building a sheepfold makes the wolf a greater enemy. . . . Ritual is not only a recurrent act, but an act expressive of a dialectic of desire and repugnance. . . . Archetypal criticism, therefore, rests on two organizing rhythms or patterns, one cyclical, the other dialectic." Northrop Frye, *Anatomy of Criticism: Four Essays* (Princeton: Princeton University Press, 1957), 106.

23. Cassirer traces the root of *templum* to the meaning "to cut," which initially described the ritual ploughing of the furrow that separated a sacred precinct from the external world and then by extension came to represent every marked-off piece of land. He compares this to the Latin word for pure theoretical thought and vision, *contemplari*, which "goes back to the idea of the *Templum*, the marked off space in which the augur carried on his observations of the heavens." *Templum* further signified bisection or intersection (as in the carpenters' use of *templum* to designate two crossing rafters or beams). This division of space into quadrants is further related to another variant of *tempus*, referring to the eastern quarter of the heavens or to the time of day this was to represent—the morning. Through this process, Cassirer has shown how "the division of space into directions and zones runs parallel to the divisions of time into phases"; and all of this occurs within the marked-off place from where the world is observed and given structure. Cassirer, *Philosophy of Symbolic Forms*, 2:100–107.

This conjunction of spatial and temporal structure relates to Eliade's observation that one of the crucial distinctions between myth and history is the way each deals with the passing of time. Myth gains its sense of reality through the emulation of paradigmatic gestures (rituals), which would necessarily be in contradiction to the linear succession of profane time, and thus requires a suspension of duration, or history. This abolition of profane time occurs, however, only within special places and only at essential periods. The rest of life passes in profane time, in undifferentiated space, and consequently is without meaning. Mircea Eliade, *The Myth of the Eternal Return*, trans. Willard R. Trask (Princeton: Princeton University Press, 1954), 35.

While both Cassirer and Eliade only imply a direction of influence in the relationship between space and time, Bergson is more explicit: "We cannot form an image or idea of number without the accompanying intuition of space. . . . We are compelled to borrow from space the images by which we describe what the reflective consciousness feels about time and even about succession." Bergson, *Time and Free Will*, 78, 91.

24. In the play performed within *A Midsummer Night's Dream*, Shakespeare introduces the character Wall: "This man, with lime and rough-cast, doth present wall, that vile Wall which did these lovers sunder; and through Wall's chink, poor souls, they are content to whisper." The wall is the device that separates the two lovers yet is also the agency by which they reestablish their relationship on even more solid ground. It is notable that what we might have anticipated as an inert piece of building becomes quite literally animated as its own implicit inside is played by one of the characters and even given a speaking role. During this brief scene the Wall is alternately hailed as sweet and lovely and then as vile, again demonstrating the wall's double capacity to separate and bring together. William Shakespeare, *A Midsummer Night's Dream*, in Shakespeare's *Twenty-Three Plays and the Sonnets*, ed. Thomas Marc Parrott (New York: Charles Scribner's Sons, 1953), 159.

25. Sedlmayr argues against the modern interest in the fluidity of perceptual connection between inside and outside that is at least one quality of the glass wall. In fact he questions the very notion that glass is able to be considered any form of walling on its own. In a critical discussion of the Crystal Palace's transparent outer skin, he writes: "What is lacking in these edifices is the notion of the separating wall or boundary between himself and the outer world which expresses man's individual assertion of himself against the universe around him." Hans Sedlmayr, *Art in Crisis: The Lost Center*, trans. Brian Battershaw (Chicago: Henry Regnery, 1958), 50.

26. Perhaps the most evocative interpretation of this liminal zone between the inside and the outside is found in Bachelard's imaginative thoughts on the secret life of closets, drawers, and wardrobes. "Wardrobes with their shelves, desks with their drawers, and chests with their false bottoms are veritable organs of the secret psychological life. Indeed, without these 'objects' . . . our intimate life would lack a model of intimacy. . . . A wardrobe's inner space is also intimate space, space that is not open to just anybody. . . . In the wardrobe there exists a center of order that protects the entire house against uncurbed disorder. . . . Order is not merely geometrical; it can also remember the family history." Bachelard, *Poetics of Space*, 78–79.

27. Heidegger believes that a location comes into existence through the agency of architecture, and therefore has no independent existence as a place within human consciousness until its presence is revealed through building. Architecture "gathers the fourfold," but in such a way that it provides it with a site. "Only things that are locations in this manner allow for spaces. What the word for space, *Raum, Rum*, designates is said by its ancient meaning. *Raum* means a place cleared or freed for settlement and lodging. A space is something that has been made room for, something that is cleared and free, namely within a boundary, Greek *peras*. A boundary is not that at which something stops but, as the Greeks recognized, the boundary is that from which something begins its presencing." Martin Heidegger, *Poetry, Language, Thought*, trans. Albert Hofstadter (New York: Harper and Row, 1971), 154.

28. Vincent Scully was one of the first historians to recognize that the Greek temple could only be understood as it engaged and set off a landscape that itself was considered

sacred by virtue of the correspondence between its own topographic structure and particular properties associated with a certain god. Thus the landscape and the temples together form the architectural whole. The Greeks had "an eye for certain surprisingly specific combinations of landscape features as expressive of particular holiness. This came about because of a religious tradition in which the land was not a picture but a true living force which physically embodied the powers that ruled the world. . . . Therefore the specific variations in form which each temple exhibits derive both from its adjustments to its particular place and from its intention to personify the character of the deity which it, too, is imagining there." Vincent Scully, *The Earth, the Temple, and the Gods* (New York: Praeger, 1969), 2–3.

Scully's views (along with those of Le Corbusier in *Vers une architecture,* and of Martienssen in *The Idea of Space in Greek Architecture*) are contrary to the more common view of Greek architecture as having little appreciation for space since the interior of the temple was seen as spatially unsophisticated. This view, however, reveals more about the modern sensibility toward the land as being only an empty site waiting to be put into service by man than it does about a sophisticated architecture that was as much concerned with the structure and meaning of places between its buildings as it was with the buildings themselves.

J. B. Jackson extends this idea to our present time in his definition of a landscape as "a composition of man-made or man-modified spaces to serve as infrastructure or background for our collective existence; and if background seems inappropriately modest, we should remember that in our modern use of the word it means that which underscores not only our identity and presence, but also our history." J. B. Jackson, "The Word Itself," in *Discovering the Vernacular Landscape* (New Haven: Yale University Press, 1984), 8.

29. A persistent theme in the writing of Heidegger is the means by which the earth is revealed and receives value through the act of building. "Mortals dwell in that they save the earth. . . . To save really means to set something free into its own presencing. To save the earth is more than to exploit it or even wear it out. Saving the earth does not master the earth and does not subjugate it, which is merely one step from spoliation." Heidegger, "Building Dwelling Thinking," in *Poetry, Language, Thought,* 150. In other words, the structures inherent to architecture connect building to the external world and in so doing reveal qualities of this world that were previously unknown. These are subsequently brought into relationship with the architecture to make a new whole. "The bridge swings over the stream 'with ease and power'. It does not just connect banks that are already there. The banks emerge as banks only as the bridge crosses the stream. The bridge designedly causes them to lie across from each other. One side is set off against the other by the bridge. . . . The bridge gathers the earth as landscape around the stream." Ibid., 152. "The temple-work, standing there, opens up a world and at the same time sets this world back again on earth, which itself only emerges as native ground. . . . The temple, in its standing there, first gives to things their look and to men their outlook on themselves." Heidegger, "The Origins of the Work of Art" in *Poetry, Language, Thought,* 42, 43. "Earth juts through the world and world grounds itself on the earth only so far as truth happens as the primal conflict between clearing and concealing." Ibid., 55.

Since the beginnings of classical philosophy there has been a slow but progressive movement away from the idea of nature as the origin and absolute exemplar for all human thought and action. For the ancient Greek thinkers, natural science was possible because of their belief that within nature was an intelligent mind that regulated its processes. By the time of Descartes, nature, as substance, was an entity separate from the mind. Each had its own intrinsic laws and processes and each was capable of acting independently of the other. With Berkeley, Hume, Kant, and Hegel, the direction of causality was reversed; now it was the mind that could constitute the idea of nature.

Nietzsche's thinking is an extension of this. Writing at a time when modern science was demonstrating just how little was actually known about the world, he could argue that the structures that we propose are in fact provisional and bear a truth that must be acknowledged as originating from human purpose rather than belonging to an immanent truth. "There is but one world, and it is false, cruel, contradictory, seductive, and without sense. . . . A world thus constituted is the true world. We are in need of lies in order to rise superior to this reality, to this truth—that is to say in order to live. . . . That lies should be necessary to life is part and parcel of the terrible and questionable character of existence. Metaphysics, morality, religion, science—in this book, all these things are regarded merely as different forms of falsehood; by means of them we are lead to believe in life. . . . In order to solve this problem man must be a liar in his heart, but he must above all be an artist. And he is that. Metaphysics, religion, morality, science—all these things are but the offshoot of his will to art, to falsehood, to a flight from 'truth,' to a denial of 'truth.'" Friedrich Wilhelm Nietzsche, *The Will to Power*, in Oscar Levy, ed., *The Complete Works of Friedrich Nietzsche* (London: T. N. Foulis, 1910). Quoted in Christopher Gray, *Cubist Aesthetic Theories* (Baltimore: Johns Hopkins University Press, 1953), 68.

It comes as no surprise that in 1889 Wilde could write: "Where, if not from the Impressionists, do we get those wonderful brown fogs that come creeping down our streets, blurring the gas-lamps and changing the houses into monstrous shadows? To whom, if not to them and their master, do we owe the lovely silver mists that brood over our river, and turn to faint forms of fading grace curved bridge and swaying barge? The extraordinary change that has taken place in the climate of London during the last ten years is entirely due to a particular school of art. You smile. Consider the matter from a scientific or a metaphysical point of view, and you will find that I am right. For what is Nature? Nature is no great mother who has borne us. She is our creation. It is in our brain that she quickens to life. Things are because we see them, and what we see, and how we see it, depends on the arts that have influenced us. To look at a thing is very different from seeing a thing. One does not see anything until one sees its beauty. Then, and then only, does it come into existence. At present, people see fogs, not because there are fogs, but because poets and painters have taught them the mysterious loveliness of such effects. There may have been fogs for centuries in London. I dare say there were. But no one saw them, and so we do not know anything about them. They did not exist until Art had invented them. Now, it must be admitted, fogs are carried to excess. They have become the mere mannerism of a clique, and the exaggerated realism of their method gives dull people bronchitis. Where the cultured catch an effect, the uncultured catch cold. And so, let us be humane, and invite Art to turn her wonderful eyes elsewhere. She has done so already, indeed. That white quivering sunlight that one sees now in France, with its strange blotches of mauve, and its restless violet shadows, is her latest fancy and, on the whole, Nature reproduces it quite admirably. Where she used to give us Corots and Daubignys, she gives us now exquisite Monets and entrancing Pissarros. Indeed there are moments, rare, it is true, but still to be observed from time to time, when Nature becomes absolutely modern. Of course, she is not always to be relied upon. The fact is that she is in this unfortunate position. Art creates an incomparable and unique effect, and, having done so, passes on to other things. Nature, upon the other hand, forgetting that imitation can be made the sincerest form of insult, keeps on repeating this effect until we all become absolutely wearied of it. Nobody of any real culture, for instance, ever talks nowadays about the beauty of a sunset. Sunsets are quite old-fashioned. They belong to the time when Turner was the last note in Art. To admire them is a distinct sign of provincialism of temperament. Upon the other hand they go on." Oscar Wilde, "The Influence of Impressionism upon the Climate," in *The Decay of Lying* (1889). Quoted in Eugen Weber, *Paths to the Present* (New York: Dodd, Mead, 1963).

The consequence of this changing valuation is significant for my argument about the boundary. The means by which it is possible to represent nature as having an intrinsic worth, as well as our willingness to act on the basis of this representation, are more issues to be faced in thinking about how we wish to inhabit the earth. The idea that nature could have an intrinsic worth is probably not understood very well. The consequences are potentially unsettling, since this worth might even be at odds with the purposes that we have defined for ourselves. Nevertheless, since we have freely elected to define our existence as separate from nature, we have elected not to live in nature but rather in relationship to it. We therefore are obligated to preserve the conditions of the earth that allow for the continued existence of an outside.

My understanding of the ideas of our "living in relationship with nature" has been significantly helped by Robert Pogue Harrison, *Forests: The Shadow of Civilization* (Chicago: University of Chicago Press, 1992).

30. "The threshold is the limit, the boundary, the frontier that distinguishes and opposes two worlds—and at the same time the paradoxical place where these worlds communicate, where passage from the profane to the sacred world becomes possible." Eliade, *Sacred and Profane*, 25. "The threshold is the ground-beam that bears the doorway as a whole. It sustains the middle in which the two, the outside and the inside, penetrate each other. The threshold bears the between. What goes out and goes in, in the between, is joined in the between's dependability. The dependability of the middle must never yield either way. The settling of the between needs something that can endure, and is in this sense hard." Heidegger, "Language," in *Poetry, Language, Thought*, 204.

31. The intervals where the plough was carried were called *portae* and became, both etymologically and defensively, the gates or portals of the city. See Fustel de Coulanges, *Ancient City*, 137.

32. "The center, then, is pre-eminently the zone of the sacred, the zone of absolute reality. . . . The road leading to the center is a 'difficult road' . . . difficult convolutions of a temple (as at Borobudur); pilgrimage to sacred place (Mecca, Hardwar, Jerusalem); danger-ridden voyages of the heroic expeditions in search of the Golden Fleece . . . wanderings in labyrinths. . . . The road is arduous, fraught with perils, because it is, in fact, a rite of the passage from the profane to the sacred, from the ephemeral and illusory to reality and eternity, from death to life, from man to the divinity." Eliade, *Myth of the Eternal Return*, 17–18.

33. Fritz Morgenthaler describes being invited to visit the home of one of the Dogon people whose village he had been studying. The trip began in a square by the entry to the village and meandered through paths both familiar and unknown. Along the way stops were made at the council place of the elders, the village chief, the house of the priest, and the place of the family elder. It was only then that a frustrated Morgenthaler was led back to the place where this strange odyssey had begun and was shown a modest house and garden within which his host lived. Although nominally his house, it could only be thought of as his home as it was shown to be a piece within a complex mosaic of places each representing quite different parts of his sense of home. Thus, the path through the city which gathered all of these pieces is also an essential piece on its own. Fritz Morgenthaler, "The Dogon People 2," in *Meaning in Architecture*, ed. Charles Jencks and George Baird (New York: George Braziller, 1969), 203.

34. In his own account of the origins of dwelling, Le Corbusier establishes an equally central role for geometry. "But in deciding the form of the enclosure, the form of the hut, the situation of the altar and its accessories, he has had by instinct recourse to right angles—axes, the square, the circle. For he could not create anything otherwise which would give him the feeling that he was creating. For all these things—axes, circles, right angles—are geometrical truths, and give results that our eye can measure and recognize; whereas otherwise there would be only chance, irregularity and capriciousness. Geometry is the language of man." Le Corbusier, *Towards a New Architecture*, trans. Frederick Etchells (1927; rpt. London: Architectural Press, 1946), 68.

35. See *Oxford English Dictionary*, 2d ed. (Oxford: Clarendon Press, 1989), s.v. "geometry."

36. Although Kline repeats the story of the origins of geometry in the resurveying of fields after the Nile's flooding, he would rather see geometry as the product of more abstract observations on the world. Morris Kline, *Mathematics in Western Culture* (New York: Oxford University Press, 1953), 16.

37. Kline conjectures that the concept of angle first came from the observation of the angles formed at the elbows and knees of the human figure. In many languages the word for the side of an angle is the word for leg or arm. Ibid.

38. In Kant's inaugural lecture as professor of logic and metaphysics at Konigsberg on August 21, 1770, he argued that space was not part of the contingent world but "subjective and ideal; and, as it were, a schema, issuing by a constant law from the nature of the mind, for the co-ordinating of all outer sensa whatsoever"(15C). "This pure intuition can be readily observed in the axioms of geometry, and in every mental construction of postulates or of problems. . . . Geometrical evidence is thus the model for, and the means of attaining, all evidence in the other sciences" (15C). Nothing, therefore, can be known of the world by the senses except that which is "in conformity with the primary axioms of space and the other consequences of its nature, as expounded by geometry"(15E). "For since geometry contemplates the relations of space, the concept of which contains in itself the very form of all sensual intuition, there can be nothing clear and perspicuous in things perceived by outer sense except through the mediation of the intuition which that science is occupied in contemplating" (15C). An

extension of Kant's logic would show that as we apprehend these principles of geometry and learn of the structure of the world, we are simultaneously learning even more about our own process of reasoning so that we might be able to act more effectively in this world. See *Kant's Inaugural Dissertation and Early Writings on Space*, trans. John Handyside (Chicago: Open Court, 1929).

39. Von Simson argues that the rise in status of architects during the Middle Ages was due primarily to their mastery of the theory of geometry. This was not, however, a case of the expected distinction between theory and practice, but instead was evidence of a purpose for architecture that was beyond even the intellectual mastery of the crafts of building. The Gothic cathedral was both a model of the medieval universe and an image of the Celestial City. Considered as an intimation of ineffable truth, the cathedral was beholden to a rigor of structural logic that was only capable of being realized through the enduring logic of geometry. Von Simson recounts how Augustine's pupil Boethius had "singled out the mason's stone ax as symbolic of an art that can only create a 'confused' shape, whereas he chose precisely the compass to represent an art that truly 'comprehends the whole.' And it was with the compass that God himself came to be represented in Gothic art and literature as the Creator who composed the universe according to geometrical laws. . . . And in submitting to geometry the medieval architect felt that he was imitating the work of his divine master." Otto von Simson, *The Gothic Cathedral: Origins of Gothic Architecture and the Medieval Concept of Order* (New York: Harper and Row, 1964), 35.

40. Cassirer sees the opposition between light and dark as fundamental to the way primitive societies constituted their world and shows how this thinking permeated many of the spatial and temporal structures erected by these societies. Cassirer, "Space and Light," in *Philosophy of Symbolic Forms*, vol. 2, chap. 2, sect. 2.

Rykwert points out that the decrees of the Roman senate were not valid if they were passed before sunrise or after sunset, and equally invalid if they were passed outside the bounds of the *templum*. He infers from this that the sunlit day is the equivalent in time to the space of the *templum*. Joseph Rykwert, *The Idea of a Town: The Anthropology of Urban Form in Rome, Italy and the Ancient World* (Princeton: Princeton University Press, 1976), 100.

Eliade's demonstrations of the way primitive cultures construed their world as an inside is similar, in that night was one of the defining qualities of the outside. Eliade, *Images and Symbols*, 38.

Bachelard makes a similar distinction but structures his polarity in section. He opposes the lit attic, with its exposed, clear, geometrical construction, with the cellar, which he characterizes as the dark entity of the house, loaded with the fears that rational thought has trouble dispensing with. Bachelard, *Poetics of Space*, 18.

41. Cassirer notes the intense sensitivity in even the most primitive cultures to important transitions from one age or status to another. Most important changes in life (daily, monthly, yearly, seasonal, and generational) are distinguished and lifted out of the uniform course of events or the monotony of the flow of time. "The fact is that long before the human consciousness forms its first concepts concerning the basic objective differentiation of number, time and space, it seems to acquire the subtlest sensitivity to the peculiar periodicity and rhythm of human life. Even at the lowest stages of culture,

even among primitive peoples who have barely arrived at the beginnings of enumeration and who consequently cannot possibly have any exact quantitative conception of temporal relations, we often find this subjective feeling for the living dynamics of the temporal process developed in astounding subtlety and precision." Cassirer, *Philosophy of Symbolic Forms,* 2:108.

42. "Where sun and moon are not considered solely according to their physical being and physical effects, where they are not worshipped for the sake of their radiance or as producers of light and warmth, moisture and rain, but are taken instead as the constant measures of time from which the course and the role of all change are read—here we stand at the threshold of a fundamentally different and more profound view of the world." Ibid., 2:112.

43. The term "rise" also means "to return to life or come back from death." See *Oxford English Dictionary,* 2d ed., s.v. "rise."

44. The convention of the north-facing map seems to be relatively modern. It was common medieval practice to orient maps of the earth toward the east so they pointed to Paradise. John Wilford, *The Mapmakers* (New York: Vintage Books, 1982), 47.

45. Rykwert gives an exhaustive account of the history and meaning of the many foundation rituals that were crucial to the form and structure of ancient Rome. If the practices he describes represent intentions about the relationship of the city to the ecological systems of its landscape and the social and political values of its citizens, the sophistication of these intentions is disturbing in comparison to the instrumentality of modern city planning. See Rykwert, *Idea of a Town.*

46. "The Roman mundus was a circular trench divided into four parts; it was at once the image of the cosmos and the paradigmatic model for the human habitation." Eliade, *Sacred and Profane,* 47.

5 Constructing the Paradigm

1. Marcus Vitruvius Pollio, *The Ten Books on Architecture,* trans. Morris Hicky Morgan (Cambridge: Harvard University Press, 1914), 10–11.

2. Ibid., 40.

3. See the *Oxford English Dictionary,* 2d ed. (Oxford: Clarendon Press, 1989), s.v. "construct."

4. As a noun, "construct" also refers to a drawn geometrical figure. See ibid.

5. "The whole does not 'have' parts and does not break down into them; the part is immediately the whole and functions as such." Ernst Cassirer, *The Philosophy of Symbolic Forms,* trans. Ralph Manheim, 4 vols. (New Haven: Yale University Press, 1955), 2:49–50. This quality of myth compares to Vitruvius's use of the term "symmetry" for the correspondence between the part and the whole whereby the part must be capable of

standing for the whole (Book 3, chapter 1). See also Hermann Weyl, *Symmetry* (Princeton: Princeton University Press, 1952).

6. The relationship between analytical and synthetic aspects of constructing is the basis of Heidegger's writing on technology. Heidegger consistently claims that technology is a human activity whose purpose is to reveal "truth." He thus sees it as both a means to something beyond itself and simultaneously a goal or end in its own right. This possible contradiction is explained through a somewhat circular argument showing that technology reveals the values or purposes of its end, but that specific directives for constructing this end are set in place only when the end is revealed. "This revealing gathers together in advance the aspect and the matter of ship or house, with a view to the finished thing envisioned as completed, and from this gathering determines the manner of its construction." Martin Heidegger, "The Question Concerning Technology," in *The Question Concerning Technology and Other Essays,* trans. William Lovitt (New York: Harper and Row, 1977), 13.

7. This purpose is further amplified by Heidegger when he examines the root meanings of *technology*. He explains that *technē* is the name for the activities and skills of the craftsman, as well as for the arts of the mind and the fine arts. Because of this convergence of craft and art, he is able to state: "*Technē* belongs to bringing-forth, to *poiēsis;* it is something poetic." Ibid.

8. See the *Oxford English Dictionary,* 2d ed., s. v. "articulate."
A further extension of this argument is suggested by the research by Frances Yates on mnemonic systems and their relationship to the structure of places. Yates shows how words, speeches, and even concepts were able to be recalled at will by classical orators practiced in the art of memory first invented by Simonides. The principles are simple. What needed recall was broken into constituent parts, with each part located imaginatively in a corresponding place within a building whose own structure and elaboration was articulate and ordered, so that the logic of how it was assembled served as the ordering principle that kept the imaginatively stored parts of the speech in their proper sequence. Visiting these places in one's imagination allowed the speech to be reassembled and delivered. The correspondence that Yates shows between articulate patterns of speech and a memorably articulate architecture shows that the logic of assembly that guides constructing is not far removed from the logic that structures the way we act in the world. Frances A. Yates, *The Art of Memory* (Harmondsworth, England: Penguin Books, 1966), 18. See also Jonathan D. Spence, *The Memory Palace of Matteo Ricci* (New York: Penguin, 1984).
In this context, Bachelard's description of the virtues of the house is notable. "Of course, thanks to the house, a great many of our memories are housed, and if the house is a bit elaborate, if it has a cellar and a garret, nooks and corridors, our memories have refuges that are all the more clearly delineated." Perhaps this is the reason that Bachelard claims that "A house constitutes a body of images that give mankind proofs or illusions of stability." Gaston Bachelard, *The Poetics of Space,* trans. Maria Jolas (Boston: Beacon Press, 1964), 8, 17.
It is also useful to compare these various uses of "articulate" to the way the same term is used in the writing of Susanne Langer on musical composition. See note 18 in this chapter.

9. Phyllis Ackerman shows how the unreflective creative imagination of primitive cultures directly emulated what they understood as the structure of the heavens in both the siting and the forms of their building. Since the weather came from the heavens, a fact deduced from the proto-scientific observations of the sky which foretold the passing of the seasons, it was reasonable to extend the implications of this to the world itself and understand it too as originating in the heavens. The prudent and practical primitive builders emulated what was understood of the structure of the heavens in order to gain some security in a world whose operations were otherwise opaque. Thus a whole category of building activity and interpretation of the land was initiated and developed that stressed the vertical connection to this source of authority. The cosmic mountain, either as found or as reconstituted in forms as diverse as the pyramid, the dome, the ridged roof, and their aedicular representations in the pediment, owes its significance to this conjunction of the practical and the mythic. Phyllis Ackerman, "The Symbolic Sources of Some Architectural Elements," *Journal of the Society of Architectural Historians* 12, no. 4 (1953), 3–7.

E. Baldwin Smith confirms this significance of the roof by noting that it was "only after solemn deliberation of the Senate that Caesar was granted the honor of having a gabled roof on his dwelling." E. Baldwin Smith, *Architectural Symbolism of Imperial Rome and the Middle Ages* (Princeton: Princeton University Press, 1956), 5.

10. For an elaboration of the themes of the aedicule see John Summerson, "Heavenly Mansions: An Interpretation of Gothic," in *Heavenly Mansions and Other Essays on Architecture* (New York: Norton, 1963).

11. In the introduction to *An Outline of European Architecture,* Nikolaus Pevsner tried to distinguish between architecture and building, giving as examples Lincoln Cathedral and a bicycle shed: the latter could not be architecture but only building, due to its lack of aesthetic appeal. While others have taken up various positions on this question, I find Norris Kelly Smith's to be most satisfactory. He argues that without any institutional meaning, building can never be considered architecture: "Palace, house, tomb, capitol, court, temple, church—these, mainly, are the buildings which stand for the institutionalized patterns of human relatedness that make possible the endurance of the city, or of society, or of the state; and these have provided almost all the occasions for meaningful architectural art for the past five thousand years." Norris Kelly Smith, *Frank Lloyd Wright: A Study in Architectural Content* (Watkins Glen, N.Y.: American Life Foundation and Study Institute, 1979), 19.

"An institution is not a person; it is an established framework, a pattern of relatedness among men, a mode of grouping within which the individual experiences membership and finds some basis for making decisions, passing judgments, determining goals. Like a building, the institution claims for itself a size and a power to endure which greatly exceed those of the ephemeral human being. By virtue of its size, its stability, and its permanence, it is able to shelter and to protect its members, not simply from the elements but from that destructive individualization, that 'scattering abroad upon the face of all the earth,' with which every urban society is in some measure threatened. A building may be said to be a work of architectural art, then, insofar as it serves as a visual metaphor, declaring in its own form something (though never everything) about the size, permanence, strength, protectiveness, and organizational structure of the institution it stands for (but does not necessarily house)." Ibid., 22.

12. "Upon the earth and in it, historical man grounds his dwelling in the world. In setting up a world, the work sets forth the earth. . . . The work lets the earth be an earth." Martin Heidegger, "The Origin of the Work of Art," in *Poetry, Language, Thought*, trans. Albert Hofstadter (New York: Harper and Row, 1971), 46.

13. Heidegger's description of the coming into existence of even so simple an artifact as a chalice indicates the complexity of the relationships among the institutional, the paradigmatic, and the material aspects of constructing. "The chalice is indebted, i.e., owes thanks to, the silver for that out of which it consists. . . . Thus the sacrificial vessel is at the same time indebted to the aspect (*eidos*) of chaliceness. Both the silver into which the aspect is admitted as chalice and the aspect in which the silver appears are in their respective ways co-responsible for the sacrificial vessel. But there remains yet a third that is above all responsible for the sacrificial vessel. It is that which in advance confines the chalice within the realm of consecration and bestowal. Through this the chalice is circumscribed as sacrificial vessel. Circumscribing gives bounds to the thing. With the bounds the thing does not stop; rather from out of them it begins to be what, after production, it will be. That which gives bounds, that which completes, in this sense is called in Greek *telos*." Heidegger, "The Question Concerning Technology," 7–8.

14. "It is this durability which gives the things of the world their relative independence from men who produced and use them, their 'objectivity' which makes them withstand, 'stand against' [Arendt explains this usage as the original and political meaning of *object*] and endure, at least for a time, the voracious needs and wants of their living makers and users. From this viewpoint, the things of the world have the function of stabilizing human life, and their objectivity lies in the fact that—in contradiction to the Heraclitean saying that the same man can never enter the same stream—men, their ever-changing nature notwithstanding, can retrieve their sameness, that is, their identity, by being related to the same chair and the same table. In other words, against the subjectivity of men stands the objectivity of the man-made world rather than the sublime indifference of an untouched nature." Hannah Arendt, *The Human Condition* (Chicago: University of Chicago Press, 1958), 137.

15. Of the many materials out of which we build, few hold the same power over our imaginations as does stone. J. B. Jackson shows that stone, with its immense age and slow maturity over the millennia, was not considered dead to primitive societies but represented a concentration of power and life and thus could express absolute reality, life, and holiness. "It is the mysterious power possessed by stone, the manner in which it linked the cosmic order with our own search for order that accounts in large part for its architectural importance." Even after tracing the shift in the lore of stone from the alchemist's search for the philosopher's stone to the chemist's analysis of properties suitable for human use, Jackson argues that this material remains significant, if not for its once hoped-for absolute permanence, at least as a reliable representation of continuity. J. B. Jackson, "Stone and Its Substitutes," in *Discovering the Vernacular Landscape* (New Haven: Yale University Press, 1984), 109.

16. Boman's provocative comparison of Greek and Hebrew thought reveals an important distinction in the manner in which Old Testament descriptions deal with issues of form, construction, and materiality. Boman notes that although Noah's ark is

described in detail, what is described is not its appearance but its construction, including very particular material specifications. He reasons that objects as such have interest in Hebrew thought not in terms of their formal gestalt but primarily as implements of human or divine action. Thus the details of assembly count for more than the completed object since these are the clues to these human actions. In the same way materials take on a different cast. Material substance is not merely something inherently empty waiting to be given form and therefore meaning, but already possesses highly symbolic properties. Consequently, materials must not lose their particularity within the whole. Boman states that "an implement is, therefore, material fashioned and used for a definite purpose." Thorleif Boman, *Hebrew Thought Compared with Greek*, trans. Jules L. Moreau (New York: Norton, 1960), 93.

The idea of a natural material having an intrinsic worth which is then revealed by the process of building is an important theme in Heidegger's thinking on technology. "By contrast the temple-work, in setting up a world, does not cause the material to disappear, but rather causes it to come forth for the very first time and to come into the Open of the work's world. The rock comes to bear and rest and so first becomes rock; metals come to glitter and shimmer, colors to glow, tones to sing, the word to speak. All this comes forth and the work sets itself back into the massiveness and heaviness of stone, into the firmness and pliancy of wood, into the hardness and luster of metal, into the lighting and darkening of color, into the clanging of tone, and into the naming power of the word." Heidegger, "Origin of the Work of Art," 46.

17. Many of the limits of antinomy derive from strict interpretation of one of the fundamental laws of logic—the law of the excluded middle. A useful discussion of this can be found in David Hackett Fischer, "The Fallacy of False Dichotomous Questions," in *Historians' Fallacies* (New York: Harper and Row, 1970), 62. For an amusing but no less useful discussion, see Peter Heath, *The Philosopher's Alice* (New York: St. Martin's Press, 1974), 114, n. 3.

18. This question of articulation has been a constant theme in the continuing discourse on architectural composition. The relationship between the elements of a structure and the structure itself was addressed by Vitruvius's observations that, in a symmetrical construct, the part is able to stand for the whole.

"In a union, every art remains itself and its portion of labour is distinct. In a mixture of different arts, or forms of composition in the same art, each one is neutralized by the rest, and its share of work decomposed. In a union the mind can enjoy the labour of each art one after the other, by means of a more or less rapid transition, and can combine in one whole, what it has viewed separately. In a mixture, every part and the whole alike escape it." Antoine Chrysostome Quatremère de Quincy, *An Essay on the Nature, the End, and the Means of Imitation in the Fine Arts*, trans. J. C. Kent (London: Smith, Elder and Co., 1837), 72.

Alberti defines this aspect of composition as *concinnitas*, whose aim is "to compose parts that are quite separate from each other by their nature, according to some precise rule, so that they correspond to one another in appearance." Leon Battista Alberti, *On the Art of Building in Ten Books*, trans. Joseph Rykwert, Neil Leach, and Robert Tavernor (Cambridge: MIT Press, 1988), book 9, chapter 5.

Compare Susanne Langer's description of musical composition. "Music, like language, is an articulate form. Its parts not only fuse together to yield a greater entity, but in so doing they maintain some degree of separate existence, and the sensuous character of each element is affected by its function in the complex whole. This means that the greater entity we call a composition is not merely produced by mixture, like a new color made by mixing paints, but is articulated, i.e. its internal structure is given to our perception." Susanne K. Langer, *Feeling and Form* (New York: Charles Scribner's Sons, 1953), 3. See also note 8.

19. See especially Arendt, "The Public and the Private Realm," in *Human Condition*.

20. Sennett's analysis of the authority that is invested in institutions shows both the desire for stability and permanence and a recognition of the improbability of satisfying this desire. "One meaning of one Latin word for authority, *auctor*, is that the authority can give guarantees to others about the lasting value of what he does. It is solid. But the social bond is no more timeless than the personal. It is historical, it cannot help but change. The strength those monuments of authority symbolize is a defiance of history, a defiance of time." Richard Sennett, *Authority* (New York: Vintage Books, 1981), 18–19.

21. My understanding of these terms and the relationships they enter into has grown out of the many public and private discussions I have engaged in with Carroll William Westfall at the University of Virginia.

22. While not wishing to misconstrue the meaning of someone who would not seem at first to be sympathetic to these arguments, I remain intrigued by Mies's comments on the free plan; what might have been a simple observation, I think, actually carries a more profound import. "A clear structure is the basis for the free plan. . . . The structure is the backbone of the whole and makes the free plan possible. Without that backbone the plan would not be free, but chaotic and therefore constipated." Mies van der Rohe, quoted in C. Norberg-Schulz, "Talks with Mies van der Rohe," *L'Architecture d'Aujourd'hui* (Paris), no. 79, 100, as cited in Christian Norberg-Schulz, *Intentions in Architecture* (Cambridge: MIT Press, 1965), 152.

23. In Smith's pioneering work on the origins and development of the dome, where he challenged the then current histories of architecture that based architectural development on changes in technology or program, he writes that the dome originated as an immaterial idea, generally bearing celestial symbolism, then became a shape and only then a constructed artifact. He thus proposes a more promising alternative to the commonly held view that the dome is the result of the constructional capabilities of stone brought to serve an a priori need: "The dome, like any other curvilinear form such as the horseshoe arch, could not have originated in cut stone, because rock is shapeless and the image has to exist in the mind of the stonecutter. Stone architecture the world over, from India to Stonehenge, began as an imitative and sculptural effort on the part of organized society to reproduce venerated forms which had formerly been constructed in more pliable materials." E. Baldwin Smith, *The Dome: A Study in the History of Ideas* (Princeton: Princeton University Press, 1950), 6–7.

24. Arnheim calls attention to the difference between a square and a circle. The former has the ability to extend beyond its own closed form due to the actual or implied intersection of lines that continue their trajectories after forming the square's perimeter.

The circle has no such possibility of extension due to its curvilinearity. Rudolf Arnheim, *The Dynamics of Architectural Form* (Berkeley: University of California Press, 1977), 86.

25. Geoffrey Scott, writing in 1914, directly challenged the Ruskinian belief in the ethical nature of an "honest" construction, proposing the complementary ideas of "fictive" construction and factual construction. Considered as independent, each of these could operate according to different intentions without the moral injunction that has continued to plague modern sensibility. Geoffrey Scott, *The Architecture of Humanism* (Garden City, N.Y.: Doubleday, 1924), 88–89.

Epilogue

1. What is also necessary to note is that Vico believed that the decay of civilization would be marked by the return of its populace to intense individual self-interest. "Thus no matter how great the throng and press of their bodies, they live like wild beasts in a deep solitude of spirit and will, scarcely any two being able to agree since each follows his own pleasure or caprice. By reason of all this, providence decrees that, through obstinate factions and desperate civil wars, they shall turn their cities into forests and the forests into dens and lairs of men." The symmetrical inversion of Vitruvius's tale is remarkable. Having regressed to that condition of solitude of spirit that both Vico and Vitruvius define as characterisitc of the wild beasts, Vico's men no longer recognize the benefits of the clearing and therefore no longer need its structures of orientation. Giambattista Vico, *The New Science of Giambattista Vico*, trans. Thomas Goddard Bergin and Max Harold Fisch, rev. ed. (Ithaca: Cornell University Press, 1968), 424.

Bibliography

Ackerman, Phyllis. "The Symbolic Sources of Some Architectural Elements." *Journal of the Society of Architectural Historians* 12, no. 4 (1953), 3–7.

Alberti, Leon Battista. *On Painting.* Trans. John R. Spencer. New Haven: Yale University Press, 1966.

Alberti, Leon Battista. *On the Art of Building in Ten Books.* Trans. Joseph Rykwert, Neil Leach, and Robert Tavernor. Cambridge: MIT Press, 1988.

Arendt, Hannah. *The Human Condition.* Chicago: University of Chicago Press, 1958.

Argan, Giulio Carlo. "The Architecture of Brunelleschi and the Origins of Perspective Theory in the Fifteenth Century." *Journal of the Warburg and Cortauld Institutes* 9 (1946), 96–121.

Argan, Giulio Carlo. "On the Typology of Architecture." Trans. Joseph Rykwert. *Architectural Design* 33 (1963).

Argan, Giulio Carlo. *The Renaissance City.* New York: Braziller, 1970.

Arnheim, Rudolf. *The Dynamics of Architectural Form: Based on the 1975 Mary Duke Biddle Lectures at the Cooper Union.* Berkeley: University of California Press, 1977.

Arnheim, Rudolf. *Entropy and Art: An Essay on Disorder and Order.* Berkeley and Los Angeles: University of California Press, 1971.

Austin, Norman. *Archery at the Dark of the Moon: Poetic Problems in Homer's "Odyssey."* Berkeley and Los Angeles: University of California Press, 1975.

Aviler, Augustin-Charles d'. *Cours d'architecture qui comprend les Ordres de Vignole.* Paris: Jean Mariette, 1738.

Bachelard, Gaston. *The Poetics of Space*. Trans. Maria Jolas. Boston: Beacon Press, 1964.

Bachelard, Gaston. *The Psychoanalysis of Fire*. Trans. Alan Ross. Boston: Beacon Press, 1964.

Banham, Reyner. *Theory and Design in the First Machine Age*. London: Architectural Press, 1960.

Barthes, Roland. "The Tour Eiffel." In *Structures Implicit and Explicit*. VIA 2. Philadelphia: Graduate School of Fine Arts, University of Pennsylvania, 1973.

Benevolo, Leonardo. *The European City*. Cambridge, Mass.: Blackwell, 1993.

Benevolo, Leonardo. *The History of the City*. Cambridge: MIT Press, 1980.

Bergson, Henri. *Time and Free Will: An Essay on the Immediate Data of Consciousness*. Trans. F. L. Pogson. 1910; rpt. London: G. Allen and Unwin, 1950.

Berry, Wendell. *The Unsettling of America: Culture and Agriculture*. 3d ed. San Francisco: Sierra Club Books, 1986.

Black, Max. *Models and Metaphors: Studies in Language and Philosophy*. Ithaca: Cornell University Press, 1962.

Blondel, Jacques F., and Pierre Patte. *Cours d'architecture: Qui contient les Leçons données en 1750 et les Années suivantes, par J. F. Blondel, Architecte*. Paris: A. Guerinet, 1771–1777.

Boman, Thorleif. *Hebrew Thought Compared with Greek*. Trans. Jules L. Moreau. New York: Norton, 1960.

Braunfels, Wolfgang. *Urban Design in Western Europe: Regime and Architecture, 900–1900*. Chicago: University of Chicago Press, 1988.

Bruschi, Arnaldo. *Bramante*. London: Thames and Hudson, 1977.

Butcher, S. H. *Aristotle's Theory of Poetry and Fine Art, with a Critical Text and Translation of the "Poetics."* 4th ed. New York: Dover, 1951.

Cassirer, Ernst. *Language and Myth*. Trans. Susanne K. Langer. 1946; rpt. New York: Dover, 1953.

Cassirer, Ernst. *The Philosophy of Symbolic Forms*. Trans. Ralph Manheim. 4 vols. New Haven: Yale University Press, 1955.

Choisy, Auguste. *Histoire de l'architecture*. 2 vols. 1899; rpt. Paris: Librairie Georges Baranger, 1929.

Coffin, David R. *The Villa in the Life of Renaissance Rome*. Princeton: Princeton University Press, 1988.

Collingwood, R. G. *The Idea of History.* London: Oxford University Press, 1946.

Collingwood, R. G. *The Idea of Nature.* New York: Oxford University Press, 1960.

Collins, Peter. *Changing Ideals in Modern Architecture, 1750–1950.* London: Faber and Faber, 1965.

Colquhoun, Alan. *Essays in Architectural Criticism: Modern Architecture and Historical Change.* Cambridge: MIT Press, 1985.

Colquhoun, Alan. *Modernity and the Classical Tradition: Architectural Essays, 1980–1987.* Cambridge: MIT Press, 1989.

Comito, Terry. *The Idea of the Garden in the Renaissance.* New Brunswick: Rutgers University Press, 1978.

Connors, Joseph. *Borromini and the Roman Oratory: Style and Society.* Cambridge: MIT Press in association with the Architectural History Foundation, 1980.

Curtis, Nathaniel Cortlandt. *Architectural Composition.* Cleveland: J. H. Jansen, 1923.

Dennis, Michael. *Court and Garden: From the French Hôtel to the City of Modern Architecture.* Cambridge: MIT Press, 1986.

Douglas, Mary. *Purity and Danger: An Analysis of the Concepts of Pollution and Taboo.* London: Ark, 1984.

Drexler, Arthur, ed. *The Architecture of the Ecole des Beaux-Arts.* New York: Museum of Modern Art, 1977.

Durand, Jean-Nicolas-Louis. *Précis des leçons d'architecture données à l'École royale polytechnique.* 1819; rpt. Unterschneidheim, Germany: UHL, 1981.

Durm, Josef, Hermann Ende, Eduard Schmitt, and Heinrich Wagner, eds. *Handbuch der Architektur.* 4th ed. Leipzig: Alfred Kröner, 1909.

Eco, Umberto. "Function and Sign: Semiotics of Architecture." In *Structures Implicit and Explicit.* VIA 2. Philadelphia: Graduate School of Fine Arts, University of Pennsylvania, 1973.

Egbert, Donald Drew, and David Van Zanten. *The Beaux-Arts Tradition in French Architecture.* Princeton: Princeton University Press, 1980.

Eliade, Mircea. *Images and Symbols: Studies in Religious Symbolism.* Trans. Philip Mairet. New York: Sheed and Ward, 1969.

Eliade, Mircea. *Myth and Reality.* Trans. Willard R. Trask. New York: Harper and Row, 1963.

Bibliography

Eliade, Mircea. *The Myth of the Eternal Return.* Trans. Willard R. Trask. Princeton: Princeton University Press, 1954.

Eliade, Mireea. *Myths, Dreams, and Mysteries: The Encounter between Contemporary Faiths and Archaic Realities.* Trans. Philip Mairet. New York: Harper and Row, 1960.

Eliade, Mircea. *The Sacred and the Profane: The Nature of Religion.* Trans. Willard R. Trask. New York: Harcourt, Brace and World, 1959.

Eliot, T. S. *Selected Essays, 1917–1932.* London: Faber and Faber, 1961.

Empson, William. *Seven Types of Ambiguity.* New York: New Directions, 1966.

Evans, Robin. "Figures, Doors and Passages." *Architectural Design* 48 (1978), 267–278.

Fischer, David Hackett. *Historians' Fallacies: Toward a Logic of Historical Thought.* New York: Harper and Row, 1970.

Forster, Kurt W. "Monument/Memory and the Mortality of Architecture." *Oppositions* 25 (Fall 1982), 1–19.

Frankl, Paul T. *Principles of Architectural History: The Four Phases of Architectural Style, 1420–1900.* Trans. and ed. James F. O'Gorman. Cambridge: MIT Press, 1968.

Frazer, Sir James George. *The Golden Bough: A Study in Magic and Religion.* Abr. ed. New York: Macmillan, 1963.

Fries, Sylvia Dought. *The Urban Idea in Colonial America.* Philadelphia: Temple University Press, 1977.

Frye, Northrop. *Anatomy of Criticism: Four Essays.* Princeton: Princeton University Press, 1957.

Fustel de Coulanges, Numa. *The Ancient City: A Study on the Religion, Laws, and Institutions of Greece and Rome.* Trans. Willard Small. 1873; rpt. Garden City, N.Y.: Doubleday, 1956.

Giamatti, A. Bartlett. *The Earthly Paradise and the Renaissance Epic.* Princeton: Princeton University Press, 1966.

Giedion, Sigfried. *Architecture and the Phenomena of Transition: The Three Space Conceptions in Architecture.* Cambridge: Harvard University Press, 1971.

Giedion, Sigfried. *The Eternal Present: The Beginning of Architecture.* New York: Bollingen Foundation, 1964.

Glassie, Henry H. *Folk Housing in Middle Virginia: A Structural Analysis of Historic Artifacts.* Knoxville: University of Tennessee Press, 1975.

Goetsch, James Robert. *Vico's Axioms: The Geometry of the Human World*. New Haven: Yale University Press, 1995.

Gombrich, E. H. "The Logic of Vanity Fair: Alternatives to Historicism in the Study of Fashions, Style and Taste." In Paul Schilpp, ed., *The Philosophy of Karl Popper*. La Salle, Ill.: Open Court, 1974.

Gombrich, E. H. *Meditations on a Hobby Horse and Other Essays on the Theory of Art*. London: Phaidon, 1985.

Gombrich, E. H. *Norm and Form*. London: Phaidon, 1966.

Gombrich, E. H. *Symbolic Images: Studies in the Art of the Renaissance*. London: Phaidon, 1972.

Gray, Christopher. *Cubist Aesthetic Theories*. Baltimore: Johns Hopkins University Press, 1953.

Guadet, Julien, and Jean Louis Pascal. *Éléments et théorie de l'architecture; cours professé à l'École nationale et spéciale des beaux-arts, par J. Guadet*. 4th ed. 4 vols. Paris: Librairie de la Construction Moderne, 1915.

Gwilt, Joseph. *The Encyclopedia of Architecture: Historical, Theoretical, and Practical*. Rev. and enl. by Wyatt Papworth. 1867; rpt. New York: Crown, 1982.

Harrison, Robert Pogue. *Forests: The Shadow of Civilization*. Chicago: University of Chicago Press, 1992.

Hawking, Stephen W. *A Brief History of Time: From the Big Bang to Black Holes*. New York: Bantam Books, 1988.

Heath, Peter. *The Philosopher's Alice: "Alice's Adventures in Wonderland" and "Through the Looking Glass."* New York: St. Martin's Press, 1974.

Hegemann, Werner, and Elbert Peets. *The American Vitruvius: An Architect's Handbook of Civic Art*. New York: Architectural Book Publishing, 1922.

Heidegger, Martin. *Being and Time*. Trans. John Macquarrie and Edward Robinson. New York: Harper, 1962.

Heidegger, Martin. *Poetry, Language, Thought*. Trans. Albert Hofstadter. New York: Harper and Row, 1971.

Heidegger, Martin. *The Question Concerning Technology and Other Essays*. Trans. William Lovitt. New York: Harper and Row, 1977.

Herbert, Robert L., ed. *Modern Artists on Art: Ten Unabridged Essays*. Englewood Cliffs, N.J.: Prentice-Hall, 1964.

Bibliography

Herrmann, Wolfgang. *Gottfried Semper: In Search of Architecture*. Cambridge: MIT Press, 1984.

Herrmann, Wolfgang. *The Theory of Claude Perrault*. London: A. Zwemmer, 1973.

Hersey, George L. *Pythagorean Palaces: Magic and Architecture in the Italian Renaissance*. Ithaca: Cornell University Press, 1976.

Jackson, J. B. *American Space: The Centennial Years, 1865–1876*. New York: Norton, 1972.

Jackson, J. B. *Discovering the Vernacular Landscape*. New Haven: Yale University Press, 1984.

Jackson, J. B. *A Sense of Place, a Sense of Time*. New Haven: Yale University Press, 1994.

Jencks, Charles, and George Baird, eds. *Meaning in Architecture*. New York: George Braziller, 1969.

Kahler, Erich. *The Disintegration of Form in the Arts*. New York: George Braziller, 1968.

Kant, Immanuel. *Kant's Inaugural Dissertation and Early Writings on Space: Selected Works*. Trans. John Handyside. Chicago: Open Court, 1929.

Kline, Morris. *Mathematics in Western Culture*. New York: Oxford University Press, 1953.

Kubler, George. *The Shape of Time: Remarks on the History of Things*. New Haven: Yale University Press, 1962.

Langbaum, Robert Woodrow, ed. *Critique of Modernity*. Charlottesville: Committee on the Comparative Study of the Individual and Society, Center for Advanced Studies, University of Virginia, 1986.

Langer, Susanne K. *Feeling and Form: A Theory of Art*. New York: Charles Scribner's Sons, 1953.

Langer, Susanne K. *Philosophy in a New Key: A Study in the Symbolism of Reason, Rite, and Art*. New York: Mentor Books, 1948.

Laugier, Marc-Antoine. *An Essay on Architecture*. Trans. Wolfgang Herrmann and Anni Herrmann. Los Angeles: Hennessey and Ingalls, 1977.

Lavin, Sylvia. *Quatremère de Quincy and the Invention of a Modern Language of Architecture*. Cambridge: MIT Press, 1992.

Le Camus de Mézières, Nicolas. *The Genius of Architecture, or, The Analogy of That Art with Our Sensations*. Trans. David Britt. Santa Monica: Getty Center for the History of Art and the Humanities, 1992.

Le Corbusier. *The City of Tomorrow.* Trans. Frederick Etchells. 1929; rpt. Cambridge: MIT Press, 1971.

Le Corbusier. *Précisions sur un état présent de l'architecture et de l'urbanisme.* Paris: G. Crès, 1930.

Le Corbusier. *Towards a New Architecture.* Trans. Frederick Etchells. 1927; rpt. London: Architectural Press, 1946.

Le Corbusier and François de Pierrefeu. *The Home of Man.* Trans. Clive Entwistle and Gordon Holt. London: Architectural Press, 1958.

Lethaby, W. R. *Architecture, Mysticism and Myth.* Intro. and biblio. by Godfrey Rubens. New York: George Braziller, 1975.

Lévi-Strauss, Claude. *The Raw and the Cooked.* Trans. John Weightman and Doreen Weightman. Chicago: University of Chicago Press, 1969.

Lévi-Strauss, Claude. *Structural Anthropology.* Trans. Claire Jacobson and Brooke Grundfest Schoepf. New York: Basic Books, 1963.

Lovejoy, Arthur O. "Nature as Aesthetic Norm." In *Essays in the History of Ideas.* New York: George Braziller, 1955.

Macaulay, David. *City: A Story of Roman Planning and Construction.* Boston: Houghton Mifflin, 1974.

MacDonald, William Lloyd. *The Architecture of the Roman Empire.* Rev. ed. 2 vols. New Haven: Yale University Press, 1986.

Martienssen, Rex Distin. *The Idea of Space in Greek Architecture: With Special Reference to the Doric Temple and Its Setting.* 2d ed. Johannesburg: Witwatersrand University Press, 1964.

Marx, Leo. *The Machine in the Garden: Technology and the Pastoral Ideal in America.* New York: Oxford University Press, 1964.

McClung, William A. *The Architecture of Paradise: Survivals of Eden and Jerusalem.* Berkeley and Los Angeles: University of California Press, 1983.

Meinig, Donald W., ed. *The Interpretation of Ordinary Landscapes: Geographical Essays.* New York: Oxford University Press, 1979.

Middleton, Robin, ed. *The Beaux-Arts and Nineteenth-Century French Architecture.* Cambridge: MIT Press, 1982.

Mitchell, W. J. T., ed. *The Language of Images.* Chicago: University of Chicago Press, 1980.

Morrish, William R. *Civilizing Terrains: Mountains, Mounds, and Mesas.* Los Angeles: Design Center for American Urban Landscape, 1989.

Moynihan, Elizabeth B. *Paradise as a Garden: In Persia and Mughal India.* New York: George Braziller, 1979.

Norberg-Schulz, Christian. *Existence, Space and Architecture.* New York: Praeger, 1971.

Norberg-Schulz, Christian. *Intentions in Architecture.* Cambridge: MIT Press, 1965.

Norberg-Schulz, Christian. "Meaning in Architecture." In Charles Jencks and George Baird, eds., *Meaning in Architecture.* New York: George Braziller, 1969.

Norberg-Schulz, Christian. *Meaning in Western Architecture.* New York: Praeger, 1975.

Novak, Barbara. *Nature and Culture: American Landscape and Painting, 1825–1875.* New York: Oxford University Press, 1995.

Onians, John. *Bearers of Meaning: The Classical Orders in Antiquity, the Middle Ages, and the Renaissance.* Princeton: Princeton University Press, 1988.

Oriard, Michael V. "Sports and Space." *Landscape* 21, no. 1 (1976), 32–40.

Ortega y Gasset, José. *The Dehumanization of Art, and Other Writings on Art and Culture.* Trans. Willard R. Trask. Garden City, N.Y.: Doubleday, 1956.

Osborne, Harold. *Aesthetics and Art Theory: An Historical Introduction.* New York: E. P. Dutton, 1970.

Ozenfant, Amédée. *Foundations of Modern Art.* Trans. John Rodker. 1931; rpt. New York: Dover, 1952.

Palladio, Andrea. *The Four Books of Architecture.* Trans. Isaac Ware (1738), intro. Adolf K. Placzek. New York: Dover, 1965.

Pérez-Gómez, Alberto. *Architecture and the Crisis of Modern Science.* Cambridge: MIT Press, 1983.

Perrault, Claude. *Ordonnance for the Five Kinds of Columns after the Method of the Ancients.* Trans. Indra K. McEwen. Santa Monica: Getty Center for the History of Art and the Humanities, 1993.

Pevsner, Sir Nikolaus. *A History of Building Types.* Princeton: Princeton University Press, 1976.

Philipson, Morris, ed. *Aesthetics Today: Readings Selected, Edited, and Introduced by Morris Philipson.* Cleveland: World Publishing, 1961.

Popper, Karl R. *The Poverty of Historicism.* New York: Harper and Row, 1964.

Porphyrios, Demetri. *Classical Architecture: The Living Tradition.* New York: McGraw-Hill, 1992.

Bibliography

Porphyrios, Demetri, ed. *On the Methodology of Architectural History*. London: Architectural Design, 1981.

Porphyrios, Demetri. *Sources of Modern Eclecticism: Studies on Alvar Aalto*. London: Academy Editions, 1982.

Quatremere de Quincy, Antoine Chrysostome. *An Essay on the Nature, the End, and the Means of Imitation in the Fine Arts*. Trans. J. C. Kent. London: Smith, Elder and Co., 1837.

Raglan, FitzRoy Richard Somerset. *The Temple and the House*. London: Routledge and Kegan Paul, 1964.

Rapoport, Amos. *House Form and Culture*. Englewood Cliffs, N.J.: Prentice-Hall, 1969.

Rasmussen, Steen Eiler. *Towns and Buildings Described in Drawings and Words*. Liverpool: University Press of Liverpool, 1951.

Reps, John William. *The Making of Urban America: A History of City Planning in the United States*. Princeton: Princeton University Press, 1965.

Robertson, Howard. *The Principles of Architectural Composition*. London: Architectural Press, 1924.

Robertson, Jaquelin T. "In Search of an American Urban Order, Part II: The House as the City." *Modulus* 19 (1989), 138–159.

Rosenau, Helen. *The Ideal City in Its Architectural Evolution*. Boston: Boston Book and Art Shop, 1959.

Rossi, Aldo. *The Architecture of the City*. Trans. Diane Ghirardo and Joan Ockman. Cambridge: MIT Press, 1982.

Rousseau, Jean-Jacques. *The First and Second Discourses Together with the Replies to Critics and Essay on the Origin of Languages*. Ed. and trans. Victor Gourevitch. New York: Perennial Library, 1986.

Rowe, Colin. *The Mathematics of the Ideal Villa and Other Essays*. Cambridge: MIT Press, 1976.

Rowe, Colin, and Fred Koetter. *Collage City*. Cambridge: MIT Press, 1978.

Ruskin, John. *Art Culture: A Handbook of Art Technicalities and Criticism*. Arranged by Rev. W. H. Platt. New York: John Wiley and Son, 1874.

Rykwert, Joseph. *The First Moderns: The Architects of the Eighteenth Century*. Cambridge: MIT Press, 1983.

Rykwert, Joseph. *The Idea of a Town: The Anthropology of Urban Form in Rome, Italy and the Ancient World*. Princeton: Princeton University Press, 1976.

Bibliography

Rykwert, Joseph. *The Necessity of Artifice.* New York: Rizzoli, 1982.

Rykwert, Joseph. *On Adam's House in Paradise: The Idea of the Primitive Hut in Architectural History.* New York: Museum of Modern Art, 1972.

Rykwert, Joseph. "One Way of Thinking about a House." *Lotus International* 8 (1974), 192–193.

Rykwert, Joseph. "The Purpose of Ceremonies: Categories of Social Action in the City and Archdeacon Frollo's Observations." *Lotus International* 17, no. 4 (1977), 57–61.

Said, Edward W. *Beginnings: Intention and Method.* Baltimore: Johns Hopkins University Press, 1975.

Schama, Simon. *Landscape and Memory.* New York: Knopf, 1995.

Scholes, Robert, and Robert Kellogg. *The Nature of Narrative.* London: Oxford University Press, 1966.

Schumacher, Thomas L. *The Danteum: A Study in the Architecture of Literature.* Rev. ed. Princeton: Princeton Archtitectural Press, 1985.

Schwarz, Rudolf. *The Church Incarnate: The Sacred Function of Christian Architecture.* Trans. Cynthia Harris. Chicago: Henry Regnery, 1958.

Scott, Geoffrey. *The Architecture of Humanism: A Study in the History of Taste.* 2d ed. Garden City, N.Y.: Doubleday, 1924.

Scruton, Roger. *The Aesthetics of Architecture.* Princeton: Princeton University Press, 1979.

Scully, Vincent. *The Earth, the Temple, and the Gods: Greek Sacred Architecture.* New York: Praeger, 1969.

Sedlmayr, Hans. *Art in Crisis: The Lost Center.* Trans. Brian Battershaw. Chicago: Henry Regnery, 1958.

Semper, Gottfried. *The Four Elements of Architecture and Other Writings.* Trans. Harry Francis Mallgrave and Wolfgang Herrmann. Cambridge: Cambridge University Press, 1989.

Sennett, Richard. *Authority.* New York: Vintage Books, 1981.

Simson, Otto von. *The Gothic Cathedral: Origins of Gothic Architecture and the Medieval Concept of Order.* New York: Harper and Row, 1964.

Sitte, Camillo. *City Planning According to Artistic Principles.* Trans. George R. Collins and Christiane Crasemann Collins. New York: Random House, 1965.

Smith, E. Baldwin. *Architectural Symbolism of Imperial Rome and the Middle Ages.* Princeton: Princeton University Press, 1956.

Smith, E. Baldwin. *The Dome: A Study in the History of Ideas*. Princeton: Princeton University Press, 1950.

Smith, Norris Kelly. *Frank Lloyd Wright: A Study in Architectural Content*. Watkins Glen, N.Y.: American Life Foundation and Study Institute, 1979.

Spence, Jonathan D. *The Memory Palace of Matteo Ricci*. New York: Penguin, 1984.

Stent, Gunther. "Limits to the Scientific Understanding of Man." *Science* 187 (1975), 1052–1057.

Stilgoe, John R. *Common Landscape of America, 1580 to 1845*. New Haven: Yale University Press, 1982.

Stübben, Hermann Josef. *Der Städtebau*. 1890; rpt. Braunschweig: Friedr. Vieweg und Sohn, 1980.

Summerson, John. *The Classical Language of Architecture*. Cambridge: MIT Press, 1963.

Summerson, John. *Heavenly Mansions and Other Essays on Architecture*. New York: Norton, 1963.

Sypher, Wylie. *Rococo to Cubism in Art and Literature*. New York: Random House, 1960.

Upton, Dell. *Holy Things and Profane: Anglican Parish Churches in Colonial Virginia*. Cambridge: MIT Press, 1986.

Van Pelt, Robert Jan, and Carroll William Westfall. *Architectural Principles in the Age of Historicism*. New Haven: Yale University Press, 1991.

Vico, Giambattista. *The New Science of Giambattista Vico*. Trans. Thomas Goddard Bergin and Max Harold Fisch. Rev. ed. Ithaca: Cornell University Press, 1968.

Vidler, Anthony. "After Historicism." *Oppositions* 17 (1979), 1–5.

Vidler, Anthony. "The Idea of Type: The Transformation of the Academic Ideal, 1750–1830." *Oppositions* 8 (1977), 94–115.

Vidler, Anthony. "Type in *Encyclopédie Méthodique*." *Oppositions* 8 (1977), 146–150.

Villari, Sergio. *J. N. L. Durand (1760–1834): Art and Science of Architecture*. Trans. Eli Gottlieb. New York: Rizzoli, 1990.

Viollet-le-Duc, Eugène-Emmanuel. *The Architectural Theory of Viollet-le-Duc: Readings and Commentary*. Ed. M. F. Hearn. Cambridge: MIT Press, 1990.

Viollet-le-Duc, Eugène-Emmanuel. *The Habitations of Man in All Ages*. Trans. Benjamin Bucknall. Boston: James R. Osgood and Co., 1876.

Vitruvius Pollio, Marcus. *Vitruvius, On Architecture.* Ed. and trans. Frank Granger. 2 vols. London: Heinemann, 1931.

Vitruvius Pollio, Marcus. *Vitruvius, the Ten Books on Architecture.* Trans. Morris Hicky Morgan. Cambridge: Harvard University Press, 1914.

Weber, Eugen. *Paths to the Present: Aspects of European Thought from Romanticism to Existentialism.* New York: Dodd, Mead, 1963.

Westfall, Carroll William. "Towards a New (Old) Architecture." *Modulus* 16 (1983), 78–97.

Weyl, Hermann. *Symmetry.* Princeton: Princeton University Press, 1952.

Wiebenson, Dora, ed. *Architectural Theory and Practice from Alberti to Ledoux.* 2d ed. Chicago: Architectural Publications, 1983.

Wilford, John. *The Mapmakers.* New York: Vintage Books, 1982.

Williams, Raymond. *Keywords: A Vocabulary of Culture and Society.* New York: Oxford University Press, 1983.

Wittkower, Rudolf. *Architectural Principles in the Age of Humanism.* 3d ed. London: Alec Tiranti, 1967.

Wölfflin, Heinrich. *Principles of Art History: The Problem of the Development of Style in Later Art.* Trans. M. D. Hottinger. 7th ed. New York: Dover, 1929.

Wycherley, Richard E. *How the Greeks Built Cities.* 2d ed. New York: Norton, 1962.

Yates, Frances. *The Art of Memory.* Harmondsworth, England: Penguin, 1966.

Zube, Ervin H., and Margaret J. Zube, eds. *Changing Rural Landscapes.* Amherst: University of Massachusetts Press, 1977.

Zucker, Paul. *Town and Square: From the Agora to the Village Green.* New York: Columbia University Press, 1959.

Index

Abstraction, 114n11
  defined, 38
  related to representation, 38–39
  typicality, 83
Action
  compared to behavior, 48–49
  and dwelling, 31
  introduced, 31
  and speech, 115n17
Architecture as text, 43, 118n29
Arendt, Hannah, 99n17, 101n6
  on the public realm, 115n17
Aristippus, 57
Aristotle, 102n9, 106n13, 107n14
  on imitation, 111n2, 113n10
Articulate, defined, 68, 133n8
Articulation, 136n18
Augustus (emperor), 4
Authority, 32
  contrasted with power, 73
  Sennett on, 137n20

Bachelard, Gaston, 122n14
  on fire, 120n7
Beginning, 21–23, 101n2, 101n6
  and Christianity, 22, 101n4
  and history, 22
  and Vitruvius, 23
Borges, Jorge Luis, 122n16
Boundary, 52–54
  and the preservation of nature, 54

Cardinal orientation, 61–62
Cardo, 62
Cassirer, Ernst, 93n4, 94n7, 101n6,
  107n14
  on space and time, 125n23
Center, 50–52, 129n32
  Borges on, 122n16
  derived from human figure, 51–52
  and entry, 56
  and the underground, 51–52
Circle, 77, 98n15
Clearing
  constituent parts, 13
  and language, 95n10
  and paradise, 97n13
  related to sky, 111n1
Collingwood, R. G., 117n24
Column, origin of, 35–36
Constructing
  and abstraction, 77–78
  analytical and synthetic descriptions of,
    67–68, 133n6
  collective stability and individual will,
    70
  defined, 66
  and discontinuity, 68–69
  Heidegger on, 133n6
  and juncture, 69
  and knowledge, 65–66
  and language, 82, 83
  and paradigm, 70
  and nature, 126n27, 127n28, 127n29